Your Cash Is
Flowing

Why every entrepreneur
needs to think like a CFO

Your Cash Is
Flowing

Why every entrepreneur
needs to think like a CFO

Kenneth M. Homza

homza
press

Your Cash Is Flowing
Why every entrepreneur needs to think like a CFO

ISBN: 978-0-9897069-0-2
Book design by Nehmen-Kodner: n-kcreative.com

Published and distributed by Homza Press
www.homza.com

To
Dad

Contents

Introduction:
Who's Your CFO?

Whether you know it or not, you do have a CFO. Someone, perhaps you, your accountant, bookkeeper, secretary, spouse, or office manager acts as your Chief Financial Officer. So the question isn't really whether or not you have a CFO (I would argue that every business does), but rather is your CFO any good at his job? Is he even qualified to be CFO?

The number of business owners I meet who tell me numbers do not matter is frightening. And almost certainly, the ones who say this are in financial trouble. Here are a few examples of what I've heard:

"I don't have a bank asking me for financial reports, so they're not important." This company had already been through corporate bankruptcy, and the owner was currently facing personal bankruptcy.

"My secretary enters all of the bills in QuickBooks and we just write the checks." Nothing wrong with that, if the person entering the bills knows what they are doing. QuickBooks is a fine

program, but if the person entering the bills puts them into the wrong account or confuses assets with expenses (and I have seen this done countless times), then how in the world would anyone know what income is earned at the end of the month?

"We don't worry about interest or depreciation every month, we let our tax accountant do that at the end of the year." I have seen businesses book a "profit" every month only to see interest and depreciation booked by the accountant in December wiping it all out and resulting in a loss for the year. Don't let any tax accountant convince you that a depreciation loss is good because it lowers your tax liability unless you also understand that you won't have enough money to invest in new capital equipment when your current stuff wears out.

"We don't look at it that way." Yes, I've actually been told by business owners that they have a better way than proven, age-old financial practices. Show me a business owner who says this and chances are they are losing money (and don't even know it).

"I don't like to look at that stuff." Really? Well, Mr. Business Owner, that "stuff" is your money (or it was before your employees wrote themselves checks that you didn't know about). Perhaps you should have paid a bit more attention, even though it's not your favorite thing to do.

Do any of these sound familiar? Is that really where you want to be? *There is a better way. Who's Your CFO?*

▶ *The rest of this book is devoted to CFO thinking in businesses from $2 million to $20 million (and beyond). Far from being a textbook, it draws on the thinking of a leading fractional CFO based upon his experiences in more than 30 companies with millions of dollars in annual revenue and hundreds of employees.*

The Case For The Fractional Chief Financial Officer

I believe the case for the fractional Chief Financial Officer (CFO) is strong. Then again, I should; I have been doing this since 2003. Put simply, the fractional CFO provides services to multiple companies at the same time. I avoid the term "part-time" because I think about every one of my clients on a daily basis even though I may be in their office for only a limited number of hours each week (or not at all).

By focusing only on the uppermost part of the value pyramid, I reserve my time for only areas where I truly add value, such as strategic direction, reporting, and key business drivers. I delegate (usually to existing staff) the more basic financial and accounting processes while at the same time I serve as a mentor to the staff to help them raise their game.

Companies with revenues in the $2 to $20 million range (sometimes higher or lower) can benefit greatly from the CFO skill set but usually don't need and can't afford a full-time resource. Moreover, there just isn't enough work to support a full-time CFO. When these companies do have full-time CFOs, these individuals are usually spending a great deal of time on basic accounting and bookkeeping matters at far too great a cost to the company. In essence, they are really not Chief Financial Officers but controllers or accounting managers with an inflated title.

For these companies, the fractional CFO is the ideal solution. It brings a critical skill set to the table, and the value added can be significant.

CHAPTER 1

Accounting 201

Yes, that does say accounting 201, not 101. The following topics aren't about the debits and credits but rather the whys and hows of financial statement preparation.

• Financial Statements Don't Mean Very Much

• Truthful Financial Results Are A Mirror

• Too Many Lines

• Update

• Don't Be Too Much Like The Big Guys

• I Love A Good Audit

Financial Statements Don't Mean Very Much

Recently I had a business owner tell me that "financial statements didn't mean anything" to him. Well, after looking at his statements, I could certainly make sense of his point of view. They were so improperly prepared that they didn't mean much to me either (except it was obvious that he hadn't been monitoring the condition of his business). Had they been properly prepared, he would have had a much better handle on how much money he was losing on a monthly basis, and we might not have been talking under a "crisis" scenario.

Financial statements should be able to tell the story of the performance of your business. At a glance, you should know whether you are making a reasonable profit or not and how that profit is translating into cash in the bank. Too often, business owners try to run their business by looking at the cash number. When the cash number starts to decline but the improperly prepared financial statements suggest that the business is profitable, they're usually perplexed.

Rather than digging in to try to unravel the situation, business owners are sometimes uncomfortable with their understanding of financial statements and choose to ignore the nagging feeling that something is wrong. They choose to believe the "evidence" of a positive number at the bottom of the income statement, usually because that is what they want to believe. The result is that they continue business as usual, waiting until they are in crisis to reach out for help. Rarely does a bad situation get better by ignoring it.

The better approach is to reach out for help in understanding your financial statements. And if the person explaining your financial statements to you cannot do it simply, concisely, and in a way that you understand, then find someone else. Don't accept the fact that you, the business owner, can't understand it. It's really not difficult, and even if it is, it's simply too important to ignore.

▶ *Do your financial statements mean very much?*

Truthful Financial Statements Are A Mirror

Truthful financial statements are a mirror. They are a reflection of what is happening in the business on a day-to-day basis. They reflect the decisions that management is making and the efficiency with which they run their business. Unfortunately, I know of too many operating executives who believe that the financial statements are something that "the accountants do."

The fact that they feel disconnected between their actions and the financial statements means that something is wrong somewhere. Maybe it's a lack of communication between operating and financial management. At times, financial results simply aren't shared, and at other times they are not shared within the proper context. Perhaps operating management is insulated by a parent organization from the economic realities of their actions. Or it might be that while short-term results appear to be good, the long-term consequences of their actions have not yet caught up with them. And then there are times when financial management takes enough actions that they make the sick patient appear relatively healthy: they stretch payables, refinance, provide intercompany loans, or find one-time gains that offset operating losses. Whatever the reason, nothing good can come from this disconnect.

If you're part of operating management, it's your responsibility to do whatever is necessary for you to fully understand the financial results of your organization. If you're part of financial management, it is your responsibility to do your very best to make sure that operating management understands the financial ramifications of their decisions.

Unfortunately, a lack of understanding of the financial results by operating management is not as rare an occurrence as one might think. I've come across a number of companies where this is the case. Often, a finance person gets a call for help when the company is in trouble. When they investigate, they find that while the company is financially troubled, the root cause of the problems is sales, operations, quality, service, delivery, or some other problem. Although it's sometimes the case that the finance or accounting staff is incompetent (which means that the debits and credits do not accurately reflect the business operations), this can almost be considered good news because it is the easiest problem to fix.

We have all heard of cases in which results are inaccurate due to misstatement of fact. Such misstatements commonly involve debates around estimates (which are a common part of complex accounting issues), but these issues are usually found in large companies where the issues are subject to legitimate debate. For smaller companies, however, the facts are pretty clear and can be easily interpreted.

▶ *Financial statements reflect the operations of the company. Use them to your advantage.*

Too Many Lines

Recently, I had the opportunity to review a few new income statements. What I saw was fairly typical: too many lines. Both statements had more than 150 line items. It is clear that the information that I reviewed is not being used to manage the business. There is just no clear organization to the income statement.

The problem is not so much the actual number of line items as the fact that they are not subtotaled into any logical order. I organized one of these income statements into 23 lines. The largest expense item was for employee costs, which accounted for 77% of total expenses (more about that later). My "all other" line item (I almost always have one of these) accounted for only 7% of total costs.

Income statements like these often fail to use account numbers. Lacking account numbers, the usual default is that the income statement is organized alphabetically. Just what are the chances that the most consequential line items in any business start with "A" and the least important ones start with "Z"? Obviously, the answer is very little.

Capturing 77% of your costs in one line item provides no detail on the single biggest expenditure of the business. Knowing that 77% of your cost is for payroll doesn't tell you anything about how those dollars are allocated across departments or activities.

I also see too many line items that just aren't material to the business. Some are so small that they have only a few hundred dollars in expenditures on an annual basis. As long as you can access the details, these should be grouped into a few larger accounts; doing so will likely provide some month-to-month consistency for forecasting purposes as well as make it easier to review each month.

Here are a few thoughts about organizing financial information in a way that is meaningful to the reader (usually the executive management team). Ultimately, the goal of these statements is to be a tool. With that in mind, I'd suggest:

- Organize around your most significant costs. Use cost centers rather than more line items if you want to understand costs by department.
- Know that you will have some miscellaneous costs but that as long as you can get to the line item detail, you don't need a line item for every $200 item.
- Use account numbers to avoid confusion between income and balance sheet items.
- Talk to your accountant about where non-operating costs should be captured. Too often these end up in the middle of the income statement. Typical examples include interest expense and interest income; I frequently see the latter in the revenue category.
- Learn how to properly record payroll expenses. These are usually booked incorrectly every pay period, and the outside CPA makes a correcting entry at year end. Why not book them correctly each payroll period?

- Book an estimated depreciation amount every month. Sure, there will be a "true-up" at year end, but you should know approximately how much fixed asset depreciation you need to cover each month.

▶ *Take a look at your financial statements. Do they make sense at a glance, or are there too many lines?*

Update

There is no better time than year-end to think about doing things differently in the new year. While I am not a big fan of New Year's resolutions (any day is a great day to start a new habit), year-end is a perfect time to update financial reporting. Finish the year with current reporting so you have a complete year of trends on the same basis. But consider beginning January with a new look to your financial reporting. The start of the new calendar year is the perfect time to decide what is working and what is not.

When developing financial reporting (accounting reports), strive to make sure that they provide meaningful information and can be easily understood by all the users. Specifically,

1. *Use meaningful accounts with intuitive descriptions.* Update them as needed to reflect the current business, not what it was 10 years ago.

2. *Make sure that cost centers reflect the organization chart* and that they link to the person who is responsible for spending. Hold them accountable to monthly results.

3. Allocate costs only where meaningful. *Avoid trivial allocations* to people who have no control over the spending.

4. *Use month-to-month reporting* so that people can see trends as they follow the columns across the page. Generally six months works well.

5. *Answer questions about the business through meaningful analysis* (examine gross margin by product line or customer, or perform fixed versus variable costs analysis, for example).

6. *Integrate any important analysis into regular reporting* where appropriate.

7. *Make reporting transparent.* It should be easy to understand how decision making and actions result in profit and loss.

8. *Simplify the process of producing the reports* by eliminating unnecessary steps and automating those that remain. Recurring journal entries are a good example. Make your accounting system work for you.

9. *Distribute your reports* to those with spending authority and to key management.

10. *Seek input from the users* about what is meaningful to them and what will help them do their jobs better.

11. Ask for or provide (depending on your role) *written explanations of changes* from prior periods (either last month or same month year ago) and changes to budget or plan.

12. *Get the entire organization focused* on a few key numbers so that everyone has an appreciation for the results of the organization.

Financial reporting is meant to be a tool that helps you drive your business forward through better understanding of revenue, margin, costs, and major financial ratios. Your reporting should provide information in a meaningful way to help drive the business to increased levels of profitability and cash flow.

▶ *In business, change is a constant. Your financial reporting should reflect those changes.*

Don't Be Too Much Like The Big Guys

For small companies, emulating the practices of "the big guys" usually has value. There is a reason why the big guys have been successful and gotten big. But they should be emulated only to a point. They have resources that the small guys don't, and that needs to be considered.

Financial statements should be treated differently in big companies versus small ones. In both, you are going for predictability and understanding, but in small companies they must be simpler and easier for the management team to understand. They must also bring about focus.

In big companies, you have a finance staff to comprehend, explain; provide variance analysis, and make sure that people are watching. Despite some notable exceptions (Enron and WorldCom, for example), big companies are actually pretty good at this. Internal financial analysts spend their days studying changes and variances and can report to senior management. They watch the income statement, balance sheet, and statement of cash flows and understand how these three statements relate to each other.

Small companies are different; they have neither the staff nor the same depth of understanding. Accordingly, their financial statements must provide more focus on key issues. Where big companies often use the balance sheet to smooth certain income statement trends, small companies should use the income statement to shine a light on period-to-period variances.

In big companies, there is a reserve booked each period for bad debt. Usually this is a percentage of sales, and it insulates any month from a large bad debt write-off. If managed properly, this is an appropriate practice. In a small company, this same practice takes the focus off the income and onto the balance sheet (which unfortunately receives only minimal attention). While it helps to match revenue and expenses, it also tends to obscure bad debt issues. Management needs to understand bad debt so that they can manage credit and customer relationships. Before deciding how to treat a problem like this in your company, consider the management team and their understanding of the issue.

I once encountered a company that accrued legal expenses monthly and buried them deeply in the SG&A (Selling, General & Administrative) line. The result was that they actually used the accrual account to put money onto the income statement when needed. They were managing results. Not only were they fooling the board, but they were fooling themselves. They didn't understand their own financial statements. I stopped this immediately. While I use this practice for predictable expenses—dividing the known cost of the annual audit by 12 is a good example—doing the same thing with an unpredictable item such as legal expenses hides the true cost from the income statement and makes a cost that is already difficult to control virtually impossible to control.

The bottom line is that financial statements are a tool. The CFO or Controller has to consider management's expertise before making decisions about the best practice of looking at monthly statements with the goal of improving that understanding over time. Of course, at year-end Generally Accepted Accounting Principles (GAAP) prevails, and monthly statements should follow GAAP as closely as possible—but with an eye toward simplicity, transparency, and understanding.

▶ *Do you understand your financial statements?*

I Love A Good Audit

To some extent, an audit is all about asking and answering questions about the financial statements of a business and whether or not those statements accurately reflect the underlying health of that business. Once, when I mentioned the audit process, the person with whom I was speaking said, "That sounds painful." I suppose some people view the financial audit process as painful, and in fact, I suppose that audits can be painful in some cases. But I think there are three essential ways to avoid the pain.

First: attitude. You have to review the audit process as an valuable feedback loop. It's an opportunity to have an objective review of the financial practices of the business and to find opportunities for improvement. If your view is to defend every journal entry you have made throughout the year so that there are no changes, then the process will indeed be painful. If, on the other hand, you view it as an opportunity to recognize another point of view and reconcile and to agree upon any differences, then it becomes about understanding your business better.

Second, it's important to accept this feedback and work it through your subsequent year's financial process. It makes no sense to have the auditors provide adjusting journal entries at the end of each year if you continue the same practices as before, only to have the auditors make the same adjustments period after period. I recently came across a company that was making payroll entries incorrectly every two weeks. When I questioned this, the person responsible said that the auditors gave them adjusting entries to fix it. I never grasp the thinking behind this process. So I asked, "What if we take 30 minutes, and I show you how to do this correctly?" She said, "That would be great. No one's ever offered to do that for me before." To me, this makes far more sense. The person doing the work learned something new and increased her skill set. Management gets a more accurate view of the financial results sooner, rather than waiting for adjustments. And we've taken an unnecessary piece of work away from the outside accountants, thereby reducing fees.

Third: have the right auditors for your company. The firm should be able to give your company the attention that you need and staff it with people who take the time to understand your business and are comfortable dealing with the level of complexity that your business entails. No one audit firm is right for all companies. The big firms tend to be overkill for the small companies, and small firms can't handle the complexity or staff the needs of Fortune 500 companies.

If your accounting firm isn't helping you move forward, I'd recommend asking business associates for referrals and interviewing other firms. Many of the companies with whom I work are small to medium size businesses with a fair degree of complexity. They need a firm that will take the time to understand the business, can handle relatively complex issues, will work hard to improve the process, and is sensitive to costs.

▶ *What can you learn from your audit?*

CHAPTER 2

Financial Planning Basics

Too few businesses operate with a financial plan, although all should. The exercise of committing their thoughts to paper forces business owners to think about what the future holds and provide a concrete measure of performance to which they can hold themselves accountable.

• Accounting Versus Financial Management

• Why Have A Financial Plan?

• Components Of A Financial Plan Should Hang Together

• Only The First Two Digits Matter

Accounting Versus Financial Management

I am constantly amazed at the number of people who can't or don't distinguish between accounting and financial management. It's no surprise, I guess. Even in big companies, the terms "accountingand finance" are often run together as if they were one word. They are not—and the differences are significant.

First, let me say that I think very highly of accountants. My brother is a Certified Public Accountant (CPA) and he's a great guy. But like most people, he has a certain area of expertise. His is audit, particularly in the financial services industry. When I have an audit or control question, I always call him. But he's not a tax expert, nor does he pretend to be.

Most companies hire a CPA for their tax expertise. They generally do a fine job with the tasks they are asked to perform, and some may even be capable of doing an excellent job of financial management. But, too often, businesses visit their CPA only at tax time with the goal of completing the necessary forms and calculating their minimum tax burden. Obviously, this needs to be done. But this job is very different from the financial management of the company.

Financial management is about understanding changes in financial performance from month to month, quarter to quarter, and so on. It also involves the daily decision making about how resources are deployed within an organization (read "resources" as "money"). This involves decisions to spend money for operating expenses and long-term capital investments or to schedule employees. Often, those running a company forget that one of their biggest controllable costs (and therefore one of their biggest levers to change the expenses of the business) is labor.

As I write this, I am looking at the financial statements for a business for the first seven months of the year. I can tell that they don't seek professional guidance to help them produce their monthly financial statements. "Raw Materials Costs" vary wildly from month to month because they charge purchases directly to "Costs of Goods Sold" without taking into account changes in inventory. Labor also varies monthly and doesn't appear to be managed tightly to the volume of business that occurs during the month. Nor do they accrue labor expenses appropriately, so a month with five Fridays has higher payroll than a month with four Fridays (sometimes this is an important consideration and sometimes it is not). Several expense line items have credits in various months, reflecting "negative" expenses and thereby distorting the income for the period. Finally, expenses that should be relatively fixed each month vary substantially.

For anyone who knows how to read financial statements, this raises multiple questions, and the answers to many will likely raise more questions. But that's precisely how one improves any company's financial reporting process—and finds increased profits in the process.

▶ *Do you have solid financial management?*

Why Have A Financial Plan?

Operating a business without a financial plan is like randomly driving around in your car and hoping to get to the right destination. Businesses need financial plans for several reasons. Banks frequently require a business plan or financial plan to support a loan or line of credit. Almost certainly, equity investors wouldn't invest without a business plan. Partners or major customers might require a business plan to ensure that you can support their growth plans. But these few examples represent *external* pressures to develop an annual plan.

But what about *internal* reasons? What about using the business plan as a tool to know where *you* are going? To judge profitability? To manage investment and resource deployment? To constantly and measurably strive for improvement? I would argue that all these reasons for developing a financial plan and financial forecast are superior to any external reason.

The true purpose of a financial plan should not be to satisfy some external requirement. Rather, it should serve as your day-to-day roadmap to success. Your financial plan should be a yardstick against which you measure successes and opportunities for improvement in your business. Comparing actual monthly results to your forecast provides a basis for asking yourself (or others) questions about the business. Where are we performing well? Are we exceeding our revenue plan in some areas while falling short in others? Which cost items are fairly stable and which seem to vary wildly or cause surprises?

Whenever I work with a new client, the business leader is almost always surprised to learn something new about the business. And this revelation almost always leads to an immediate action plan to do something differently. Sometimes it leads to a serious review of monthly operating costs and an examination of each expenditure to determine whether it adds value to the business and is truly necessary. Other times, we see areas of strong performance that may not have shown through the overall results without digging deeper or comparing results to expectations. But it always leads to action. And action drives improvement.

It's not just big businesses that can benefit from building a financial plan and reviewing it on a regular basis. It's a sure bet that your business can benefit as well.

▶ *Take time to develop a business plan and learn where your business is going.*

Components Of A Financial Plan Should "Hang Together"

Given the importance of having a financial plan as a roadmap to achieving desired levels of profitability, I now want to discuss the components of your plan.

There are many books, software programs, and outlines that lay out the components of a business plan. Some are good; some are not so good. But what I find most important about any plan is whether or not it is internally consistent and cohesive. In other words, does it "hang together?"

At one point during my career, I was responsible for presenting the company's financial plan to major investment banks. I remember one meeting in particular, during which an investment banker took the time to point out that the numbers he saw in the financial plan agreed precisely with those that had been presented by the VP of Engineering. Frankly, I was surprised that he took the time to mention something that seemed so obvious. "Of course they agreed," I thought. "We work for the same company and talk on a regular basis." But the investment banker told me that rather than being common, this was unique. Often, executives or managers of different departments have varying views about the resources required to deliver an agreed upon objective (or they don't even agree on the objective), and nowhere does this become more evident than in the financial plan. The result is a business plan that doesn't "hang together." This is almost always obvious to an experienced reader, and it's a sure sign that not everyone in the organization is on the same page.

The very process of developing a plan for your business should involve active discussions of various points of view. Through these discussions, components of your plan (marketing, operations, research, product development, customer service, selling effort, pricing, and so forth) will be debated, and afterward either a decision will be made or consensus will be built (depending upon the decision making process at your company).

What should emerge is a common point of view about the goals and the necessary steps to get there. This is the true power of having a roadmap for your business and an area where your CFO should play a key role. To truly add value, this person must understand every function of the business, keep an eye out for inconsistency, and work tirelessly to resolve disputes.

▶ *Do you have a plan that "hangs together"?*

Only The First Two Digits Matter

I spend a fair amount of my time developing financial forecasts. As you approach year-end, everyone should be starting to think about the next year. What are expected revenues? What changes will we make in our cost structure (by either necessity or choice)? What will the bottom line look like compared to the current year?

This effort is, or should be, one of collaboration. Generally, the finance person responsible for actually producing the forecast should be receiving input from sales, marketing, service delivery, administration, production, research and development, the executive team, and perhaps even the board of directors with respect to their thoughts about the upcoming year (or perhaps multiple years). Furthermore, it is best that this input be shared openly as opposed to being sent only to the finance person. This allows each person the opportunity to challenge the assumptions of every other person and to make sure that everyone is on the same page. It's vital that if the plan calls for a 10 percent increase in revenue versus the prior year, for example, everyone is planning their resources accordingly.

As you move through your planning process (either as the person responsible for pulling together the forecast or as a participant), it's necessary to step back, think strategically, and not allow yourself to get mired in the details. Think about what is happening within your company, the competitive environment in your industry, and economic factors generally.

I like to say that only the first two digits matter. Why? Because we are dealing with a forecast. By its very definition, it is an estimate, and therefore it will be wrong at least to some extent. The question isn't whether the forecast is wrong but rather by how much? I have seen people spend an inordinate amount of time trying to be precise in their forecast but miss the big picture. Too often, I'll see people develop extremely complex formulas to forecast a line item without thinking about the big picture. To develop a forecast without considering the context of historical trends, volume, and "the bigger picture" is a recipe for disaster.

While I don't mean to suggest one should not sweat the details, it's also beneficial to keep in mind that time is a finite resource, and it's important to focus your efforts where they will have the most value.

If you are forecasting an expense line item of some $50,000, then the digits after the initial comma are neither material nor predictable. The same applies even if you are forecasting a profit picture of $10,500,000 dollars. In that case, even though the potential value of whether that "5" after the first comma ends up being a 1 or a 9 is significant, one's ability to forecast it is relatively small. For new businesses, even getting the first digit of the revenue forecast right can be a challenge.

If you are paying attention to how your forecast relates to prior periods, percent to revenue, month-to-month trends, industry norms, and external factors, then you'll probably end up with a forecast that is reasonable.

▶ *Focus on the digits that matter.*

CHAPTER 3

Measuring The Business

Measurement is the key to business. As they say, what gets measured gets done. Developing a set of key metrics and a regular schedule of understanding your business performance against those metrics will likely result in a marked improvement of profitability.

• Key Indicators Force A Business To Maintain Focus

• It's Mid-Year . . . Are You In Control?

• Step One

• It's Monday Morning: How'd Your Business Do Last Week?

• Is $10 Real Money?

• Keep The Pressure On

Key Indicators Force Businesses To Maintain Focus

As stated earlier, the components of a financial plan should "hang together." Once you've developed a financial plan and your executive team has reached a consensus, the challenge becomes implementation. One of the biggest challenges that many companies face is staying on track by focusing on the right things.

There are many reasons companies lose focus. Perhaps the most common are the day-to-day crises that affect any business. Customers have emergencies, equipment breaks, employees are out sick, executive management seems to change priorities, and personal priorities get in the way. The list seems endless. Priorities set during the planning process can get lost in the shuffle. The energy that was generated immediately upon completing the financial plan can seem like a distant memory.

One way to prevent this is regular and consistent review of results versus goals. While we generally think in terms of financial goals being reviewed at the end of the month, there are more immediate goals that we can review as well. Often, companies refer to these as *Key Business Drivers* or *Weekly Performance Metrics.* Whatever they are called, they are meant to be early indicators of whether you are moving toward your long-term business goals. They are measurements of the overall health of your business.

Examples of potentially meaningful performance metrics include:

- Sales calls made during the week
- Number of customer complaints
- Refund dollars given
- Percentage of up (or down) time for a particular process, system, or machine
- Lost time because of injury
- New customer orders
- On-time shipments
- Number of shipments per day or per shift

The list is seemingly endless, but the point is finding a reasonable number of key measurements that tell you how your business is doing on a daily or weekly basis.

At one point in my career, I worked for a retailer who could look at the shipping dock on Monday morning and tell me the weekend sales number. After a while, I could do it, too. I'm willing to bet that you can think of indicators that are truly consequential to your business and that tell you whether things are going well or poorly even before your financial statements are produced.

In a recent client meeting, key management and I determined that the difference between profit and loss was that the company was shipping one less load per week than in the past. With this knowledge, the company can know every Friday whether they've had a successful week or not. More important, it gives them a very measurable goal on which to focus.

If you can find the key performance metrics that affect your business, then the monthly financial statements won't contain any surprises. You'll know how your business is performing every day and have a clear expectation of month-end results.

▶ *How do you maintain focus?*

It's Mid-Year: Are You In Control?

In the United States, the July 4th weekend represents a summer holiday and the perfect time to reflect on business performance during the first half of the year. Whenever you reach your mid-year, it's an opportune time to assess whether you are on track to meet your goals and objectives or if you need a mid-year course correction.

This is an ideal time to look at the first half of the year and ask whether results were good enough. How did they compare to your plan? Could your company or division have done better? Could you, personally, have performed better? Did you meet your goals, exceed them, or fall short? Or did you merely react to the daily issues that crossed your desk?

I have some friends with whom I used to regularly ski in Colorado. At the end of a run, we'd ask each other "Did you ski the mountain or did the mountain ski you?" Of course, we all made it down the mountain, but what we were really asking each other was whether we were in control of our path or we were reacting to the bumps, trees, ice, fellow skiers, and other obstacles.

Ask yourself the same question about the first half of the current year. Were you in control of your path down the mountain or did you spend most of your time reacting? In skiing, as in business, you can't control your path by reacting to the pressures of the moment. Rather, you need to be looking two or three moves ahead and planning your next move well before the time comes to execute it.

Ask yourself how the second half of the current year can be better. What plans, systems, or measurements can you put in place today to ensure that you or your business perform better in the second half of the year than in the first half?

If you're doing a good job of planning today, challenge yourself to make it better. If you're not doing any planning or goal setting, set some short-term goals and make a plan to achieve your desired results.

▶ *To control your path, whether in skiing or business, you need to plan ahead.*

Step One

I sometimes wonder whether all the computing power that has been applied to business over the last 30 years has produced any better information. Yes, we have reams of data, but there are times when they serve very little purpose because they are not organized into useful information.

For example, I can think of two recent client companies that produced reports that weren't of much value. In one case, there was an income statement that was poorly organized and couldn't produce meaningful customer profitability information. In another case, there was a summary of weekly activity that could not be reconciled to resources deployed. Even if you understood this report perfectly, it would do little to help you to understand the business.

So, step one is to develop *meaningful* reporting for your business. If you do not have information at hand today, I can assure you that this step will not help your business this week. (Yes, I said "not.") Generally, useful business information is the result of looking at trends over time and developing comprehension of the relationships between key pieces of information. In my opinion, it takes a half-dozen time periods (six weeks of activity reporting and six months for income statements, for example) to start to draw meaningful conclusions. But I have almost always found that, once you start to look at this information, you will see trends and ask questions that will lead to ways to improve the business.

In the case of the poorly organized income statement, we started at the beginning of February and reorganized effective January 1. When we closed June, we had six months of good data. Yes, the first several months were difficult, because it felt like we took a step backward. We had *no* trend information, where previously we had bad trend information. But even that could be considered an improvement. Bad information serves no purpose other than to distract at best and to mislead at worst.

In the other case, the one with the unhelpful weekly activity summary, we started fresh the first week of July. By the end of July, we had enough information to affect the business and generate a better result (increased profits) in the third quarter.

One of the reasons that I believe people don't focus on better reporting is that the result lacks immediacy. It is highly unlikely that working on better reporting the first week of July would solve any problems before the Fourth of July break. We tend to be so short-term focused that we spend the majority of our time considering the problems of the day as opposed to activities that will benefit us in the long run. But that doesn't mean it's not worth the effort to focus.

Given that it is going to take six months for you to develop good income statement reporting, if you start today you'll probably be able to identify opportunity areas in your business in three months and have good information in six months. That will allow you to move forward with a strong basis of information and to plan to be more profitable in next fiscal year.

Every day you wait is opportunity (and profits) lost. Don't delay. Take step one today!

It's Monday Morning:
How'd Your Business Do Last Week?

A month can be a long time for a business, especially one that is struggling. Some businesses I've worked with, especially the more successful ones, produced weekly operating statistics presented through reports such as Key Business Drivers, Flash Reports, and Monday Morning Reports. Regardless of name, the focus of each was the same: providing insight into the results of the prior week. The statistics varied (appropriately so) depending upon the kind of business. But there are many kinds of things that all companies can know at the beginning of every week or even more frequently:

- Sales
- Traffic (people coming into a retail store location)
- Conversion (percentage of potential customers that purchase)
- Product mix (premium versus base product)
- Number of customers served
- Customer complaint calls (or compliments)
- Shipments (units, dollar value, on-time, late)
- Average sales per customer or transaction

- Calls or appointments made by the sales team
- Proposals submitted to customers (and their dollar value)
- Win or close ratio for sales people
- Orders
- Customer satisfaction results
- Advertising spending
- In-bound calls or Web clicks in response to advertisement or promotion
- Estimated gross margin dollars or percentage
- Cash collected
- Change in receivables
- Employee absenteeism or hours worked (or billed for professional service firms)
- Factory or production output
- Efficiency measures

If you think about your business, I'm sure that a few of these statistics would be meaningful to you. And I have no doubt that there are others you could add in order to have a handle on the pulse of your business. Start with a few and build from there.

▶ *How'd your business do last week?*

Is $10 "Real Money"?

Increasing daily performance is like compounding interest.

While the results of any one day may not seem significant, the benefit to your business can be significant over the long run. What if you found a way to increase profits or save just $10 per day starting January 1? That doesn't sound like much, does it? But by the end of the year, your profits would have increased by $3,650.

What if you could find another $10 per day the next year and the year after? In five years you would have increased your annual profit by $18,250 ($3,650 x 5). Now, what if you plan on selling your business? While multiples vary by industry, economic conditions, and a host of other factors, let's just assume that you sold your business for five times annual profits or cash flow. You would have added $91,250 ($18,250 x 5) to the value of your business. *That's nearly $100,000.*

Obviously, my $10 example is simply an illustration. But I think it makes a point. I've met many business owners whose attitudes seem to be that the small dollars don't really matter and that only the big items matter. While I would certainly agree that you should spend more time making a $10,000 decision than a $10 one, it's also key to remember that small dollar decisions add up over the long run.

Sometimes those little financial matters are recurring monthly expenses that go overlooked. You can grow accustomed to them as a cost of doing business. But are they really necessary? Sometimes they're not even small items. They can be hundreds to thousands of dollars per month that have crept into the company's spending pattern and can be overlooked.

While it's important to ask how monthly expenses compared to the month prior, it's just as important to ask whether every expense is necessary. What are the consequences to the business if the expense were reduced or eliminated? If you look closely at your business, I'll bet you can find a few expenses that were necessary at one point but are no longer justifiable.

Perhaps more important, small financial decisions can send a message to others in your organization about spending. If no one is being vigilant about expense control, it's easy for everyone to be complacent.

Just like snowflakes, those small dollar decisions add up and can be either a thing of beauty (when carefully controlled) or a disaster waiting to happen. Never overlook an opportunity to question and decipher expenses.

▶ *So, is $10 real money? I'd argue that it certainly can be.*

Keep The Pressure On

I have suggested that you look at key business indicators on a weekly basis, but that may not be enough: I also advise that you keep the pressure on by consistently setting financial and operational goals and following up on those goals.

Over the years, I've talked with many executives about the value of good follow-up. While many of us have heard complaints from staff about the value and need for follow-up on business matters, we've found a high correlation (admittedly anecdotal) between the incidence of tasks being completed and good—some would argue relentless—follow-up activity. The simple fact is that people respond to appropriate pressure to accomplish tasks. If they know that someone will be checking in to see that a task is completed, they are much more likely to finish that task. People respond to deadlines, or, as one executive I know puts it, "People respect what you inspect."

Tasks, goals, milestones, deadlines—you choose the term— are ultimately reflected in financial performance. If you are striving to meet day-to-day operating goals, you will *definitely* see the results in your monthly financial statements.

The monthly financial review process is a perfect time to talk about overall goals and accomplishments. If it was a process improvement task, it will almost certainly show up as a cost savings (or lack thereof, if not accomplished on time). If it was a prospecting or sales goal, it will show up as increased revenue (or lack thereof). If it were a new project, program, or R&D activity, it may show up as a lack of spending (that, too, can be bad if resources that were to be invested for future benefit are not appropriately spent). If it was a collections goal, it will show up on the balance sheet as too high a level of accounts receivable and too little cash.

Are there goals that won't affect the financial statements on a monthly basis? Sure. Saving a couple of hours of staff work won't necessarily show up as a cost savings from one month to the next. But over time, these will show up as you hire more people to implement inefficient processes.

In other words, every goal or objective your company has, or doesn't have, will eventually have an impact on the financial statements, either positively or negatively. If you keep the pressure on your team to consistently achieve their goals, the results will show up positively in the financial statements. If you don't, then the results will show up negatively.

Either way, properly prepared financial statements will tell the story about how consistently you keep the pressure on to achieve business results.

▶ *The choice is yours. Do you use your financial statements to keep the pressure on?*

CHAPTER 4

Make Action Count

You look around your business and people are busy but nothing is getting done—at least not the important stuff. Are your people doing the right things? Are you?

• Are You Busy Or Bored?

• 33.33 Percent Of Life Is Just Showing Up

• What's The Result?

• Water The Plants

• What Got You Here Won't Get You There

Are You Busy Or Bored?

Are you busy or bored at work? It's a question worth asking, and the answer can probably give you insights into your company's financial position even if you've never seen an income statement or balance sheet.

If there never seems to be enough hours in the day to get your work done, odds are that your company is staffed appropriately and is profitable. This is especially true if you look back several years and realize that you and those around you are doing more with less, have improved processes, and are more efficient than you were several years ago. Frankly, this is what it takes just to stay even with the competition in the marketplace.

If you're bored at work, and you can tell that others around you are bored, chances are that your company is struggling financially. Regardless of your role, you'd better be busy enough that you're adding value well beyond your salary. And I don't mean 10% or 20% more. That is not even enough to cover employment taxes and fringe benefits. I'm talking about adding value of 2, 3, 4, 5, or even 10 times your salary. Depending upon your industry, that's what it takes to pay for corporate overhead, capital investment, and to earn a fair return for the shareholders who have invested in your company.

If you and those around you are bored, you'd better do something about it because one of two things is going to happen: either someone is going to realize it and single you out as an opportunity to reduce costs, or your company will not survive much longer. It may take months, even years, but eventually the company will wither and die. Even if it doesn't go out of business completely, it will be a lifeless place where people are just showing up and going through the motions. One way or the other, sooner or later, chances are that you'll end up unemployed.

I recently heard about a factory worker who was frustrated about his plant's closing. At the same time, he admitted to being bored at work and "hardly working" for years. What's amazing is that he really didn't make the connection that it was his own lazy performance and that of the people around him that brought about his state of unemployment. Sure, he held on to a job longer than he should have, but no company can survive indefinitely when a large percentage of its employees are unproductive.

Whether you make $20,000, $200,000, or $2,000,000 per year, you have to add more value to the business than you're taking out for the company to survive.

So, as you go about your next workday, ask yourself if you are busy or bored. Ask yourself if there are ways that you and your coworkers can add more value to the business. Adding value is the best way to ensure continued employment because you will be working for a profitable company.

▶ *Busy or bored. Think about it.*

33.33% Of Life Is Just Showing Up

Woody Allen famously said, "90% of life is just showing up." While I'm not sure what the exact percentage should be, I'd argue that it's actually no more than one-third. Showing up is necessary, but it's rarely sufficient.

Amazingly, there are times that people don't even bother to show up. And I mean this quite literally. I've seen people go through the interview process, get the job, and then just not show up on the first day of employment. If I hadn't seen it more than once, I'd have assumed it was a fluke, but it's not. It just makes me wonder what people must be thinking.

Whatever you are doing, it's worth doing more than just showing up. You only get out of any endeavor what you put into it, and it takes more than a minimum performance in order to be successful.

So rather than thinking that 90% of life is just showing up, perhaps it's more reasonable to think that 33.33% of life is showing up, 33.33% of life is preparing, and 33.33% of life is about being in the moment and fully engaged in the task at hand.

I used to train in karate. (I hate saying "used to.") I can assure you that karate is a pursuit for which just showing up won't cut it.

It might surprise many to know that when training in karate you never get hit. Really, it's true. Rather, you fail to block a punch or kick from an opponent. While the result is the same—ending a class bruised and battered—the attitude that the philosophy instills is quite different. It's not about being there and something happening to you; it's about being responsible for what happens.

Business is a mix of preparation, being in the right position, and execution. As you think about your business, think about the areas where people, departments, divisions, and so forth perform as though they believe that 90% of life is just showing up. These are areas of opportunity where you can improve performance.

▶ *Remember, only 33.33% of the life of your business is just showing up.*

What's The Result?

No matter the status of your business, new strategies are needed for you to take it to the next level. One frequently used management tool that is used to gauge action is to ask an employee, "What are you doing?" The more critical question really is, "What's the result of what you are doing?"

If you're working at Acme Tire & Auto Centers installing tires, for example, the link between action and result is pretty clear. Once the tires are installed and the car is off the lift, the customer is going to pay the bill and Acme will have earned revenue (and profit margin, assuming that they have a good awareness of their costs and have priced their product appropriately).

But many of us work in office environments, where the link between tasks and results can be far less clear. To further complicate matters, the link between an employee's action and what that person is actually doing can be almost nonexistent. While it's pretty easy to see what the person at Acme Tire is doing, it's often not possible to tell what the person sitting in front of a computer is actually doing. It could be anything from pertinent work to playing solitaire (the latter being one of the reasons managers ask, "What are you doing?" and are comforted by any answer that sounds like work).

But I would suggest that it's far more critical to consider the value of the tasks being performed, not just whether they fit into the broad category of "work." After all, that is the category in which the vast majority of time (and therefore dollars) is spent.

If someone in marketing is sending out a direct mail campaign, management should know the response rate, the number of eventual customers, and the resulting profit margin. How do these numbers compare to the cost of the campaign itself?

If someone is producing a report, then management should understand both how that report is used in decision making (assuming that it is used) and the cost of producing it. In large companies, a common way to learn how reports are used is the "scream test": someone stops sending out the reports and simply waits to see who screams about it. It's remarkable how little screaming is actually heard.

So, instead of asking, "What are you doing?" consider adding, "And what is the result?" How does it add value to the company? Does it directly generate revenue or lower expenses? Does it fulfill some regulatory need? Does it provide valuable information to management to enable decision making? Does it serve the customer?

▶ *Take a moment to ask yourself and those around you: What are you doing? What's the result?*

Water The Plants!

B elieve it or not, one of the first things that I look for when I walk into an office is whether anyone waters the plants. While I care about the health and welfare of the plants, what I am really looking for is whether anyone goes above and beyond to take care of little things that are usually not in anyone's job description. It immediately gives me a sense of the organization.

In any company, there are responsibilities that fall outside of job descriptions. No job description anticipates everything that happens or is supposed to happen every day. And while most job descriptions have a category for "all other duties," it's how people actually interpret those catch-all assignments that determine how an organization functions.

Small mistakes, often at the lowest levels of the organization, can take significant time and energy to fix, and the fixing usually is undertaken at a much higher level in the organization. Fundamentally, it's people taking care of problems early, before they turn into major dilemmas, that allows everyone in the organization to perform at the highest possible level. The further down the organization chart that a problem can be solved, the more effectively that organization can operate.

Organizational performance is governed by the performance of every individual within it. It doesn't matter how great a sales superstar you might have in your company if the people responsible for delivery aren't doing their job effectively, because customers will eventually get tired of dealing with the organization's incompetence and find another source. And if that sales superstar has to step in and fix problems, the time spent doing that can't be devoted to making more sales.

Everyone in the organization has only so much "bandwidth." Every time employees are forced to deal with problems that could have been handled further down in the organization, they are not operating at their highest level of efficiency or making the best use of their time. This limits not just their effectiveness but the company's ability to achieve its full potential.

I can cite countless examples of people being forced to dive down into the organization to deal with something that could have and *should* have been handled by another resource. As a fractional CFO, my job is not only to oversee the finance function but to take things off the plate of the CEO and other executives so that they can manage the tasks that they are uniquely qualified to handle.

Watering the plants is just an example of day-to-day functions that need to happen smoothly for an organization to achieve its potential. So the next time you walk into your office, do more, so that everyone else can, too.

▶ *And notice who waters the plants, they probably over deliver in other areas as well.*

What Got You Here Won't Get You There

Those are words worth thinking about. When I heard them recently, they struck me, in part because it was at a 6:00 a.m. boot camp run by Keath Hausher, president of Shark Fitness Training. When you're working out at that hour of the morning with about 50 other people, you have the sense that you are doing everything you can to stay healthy. But to be truthful, I've reached a plateau. And to get to the next level, whatever that is, I have to do more.

The same is true in business. The actions you have taken to get where you are today will not get you to the next level of success. To measurably improve consistently, you're going to have to do more. Whether your business is performing well or poorly, taking different actions is the key to changing your result.

Think about your business and the number of things that you are doing "the way they've always been done." Some of those may be fine, but people, practices, and processes may have long since served their purpose and may actually be holding you back.

- *Reports that once served to answer a key question are still being produced even though the question may be irrelevant.* New ways of reporting to answer questions of the day may not have been instituted because the old stuff is taking up so much time.

- *Processes that seemed efficient yesterday may seem slow today.* It wasn't that long ago that fax machines were the fastest way to send information. Now, it seems we only fax something when someone doesn't have access to their email.

- *Finally, employees who were vital to the business in its early stages may not have grown with the company and may now be holding the company back.* Not everyone grows with an organization. The top marketing person for a $1 million dollar business might not be the right person when that same business reaches $10 million, $20 million, or more.

There is a difference between staying the course and staying in a rut. In any endeavor, to move to the next level you have to challenge yourself and those around you to do more than you did yesterday. In business, competition is fierce, and you can be sure that your competitors are trying to pass you by. Don't make it easy for them. Challenge yourself to stay one step ahead and move to the next level.

▶ *What are you going to do differently today?*

CHAPTER 5

A Broken Cog Slows All Wheels

In this chapter we look at the business as a system. If one part of that system is broken, it affects every other segment of the business.

• It's A System

• The Voting Process

• Fix Your Small Problems First

• The Ripple Effect

• Simplify

• Strive For Perfection

It's A System

A business is a system. Much like a mechanical system or a biological system, if one part is not working it puts pressure on all the others. If you think about your own business this way, I'll bet you'll find that it's true.

As I tend to get calls from businesses that are struggling, I probably see this more than most. The breakdown of a business system shows up in the numbers, but finances are a reflection of the way the business functions. Show me a business that functions smoothly and efficiently, and it will likely be profitable. Show me one that struggles with day-to-day problems and I'll bet that the financial performance will reflect that as well.

While every business is different, most have these key functions:

- Sales (closing the deal)
- Marketing (getting the word out)
- Customer service (resolving problems or providing support)
- Product (actually producing a product or delivering a service)
- Accounting/finance (in its simplest form, this means adding up the numbers)

- Information technology (keeping us all connected)
- Management and administration (overseeing all the other functions)
  - Your business might also have Research and Development or some other functions.

Now, imagine if one of these functions just stopped. Think about it: if no one delivered your product or service, revenue would dry up pretty quickly. If accounting didn't send out bills and receive payments, the bank account would soon be empty. If the sales department doesn't close new business, the top line will drop. Even if building services quit emptying the wastebaskets and cleaning the office, the place would soon become a mess, and that would affect the entire organization.

Clearly these examples are extreme. It would be highly unusual for an entire department to just stop working. However, it's not so uncommon for departments to be operating at less than full capacity and maybe not even meeting minimum job requirements. When this happens, it puts pressure on every part of the organization.

When the sales department isn't making its goals, profits drop. This may result in a cutback on resources and make it harder for those delivering products or services to do their jobs. Accounting may stretch payables. This results in calls from unhappy vendors. This takes time and further affects the organization's ability to get the job done.

Maybe those delivering the product or service don't do a good job, and sales suffer as a result. Customers may withhold payment. There will be more complaint calls. Management will step in to deal with the problem of the day rather than devoting their time to planning for the future.

The problem can start anywhere. When you see it, it's not so much about where it started as it is about getting a handle on it and stopping it. Of course that is easier said than done. If you're fortunate enough to see a problem starting, nip it in the bud, because it won't take long for it to infect the entire organization. If your business is struggling, think of it as a system. You might get a new perspective.

▶ *Stand back and observe the processes in your business. You'll probably learn a lot.*

The (Voting) Process

Think about the most recent presidential election. Consider everything you thought about as you headed to the polls and the process you went through that day.

Some of us were fortunate enough to go to polling places with short lines, but many of us had a bit of a wait (a small price to pay for the privilege of voting). But as I stood in line that afternoon, making small talk with the people around me, I couldn't help think about the process that was going on in front of me. During the hour I was waiting, I noticed that there were always at least six voting machines open. Clearly the availability of voting machines didn't seem to be the problem that was holding up the line. I looked at the six stations that were designated for certain letters of the alphabet (A-D, E-H, and so on). These weren't busy, either. Finally I looked at the first station. There was one person looking at everyone's voter ID card, making a few notations on a slip of paper, and handing it to them. This person wasn't comparing voter ID cards to any list but just looking at the voter ID card and handing out a slip of paper to be taken to the next station. This was the bottleneck. I wondered what was the purpose of this task. Was it essential to the process? Could it be eliminated? Why couldn't there be two people performing it? Couldn't we computerize this process? How about voter cards with a magnetic strip? In a time when almost every task in our lives has some association with computers, couldn't something be done to improve this process?

My aim here is to point out the value of standing back and observing the processes in your business. Too often, we are so busy facing the day-to-day challenges in our businesses that we fail to take the time to stand back and simply observe the processes. Given the opportunity, you can often find improvements by asking the simple question: *why?*

Force yourself to take some time away from your desk. Stand back and observe what happens day to day. If you don't think that you can be objective, ask a trusted friend or colleague to do it for you. I have little doubt that you'll find opportunities for improvement if you spend the time to look at the processes in your business.

▶ *What process can you fix today?*

Fix Your Small Problems First

Many books have been written about prioritization and tackling the A's before the B's and C's. Still, I think there is a certain logic to tackling small problems first. I'm talking about real problems, not cleaning your desk and sharpening pencils so that you'll be ready to tackle the big problems. That kind of activity is simply procrastination. I'm advocating a strategy of dealing with small problems before they become big problems.

Ask yourself if it is more likely that a small problem will go away or become a big problem later. I think we all know the answer. Just in case you need a few examples to get you started, consider these:

- Have you ever seen a minor roof leak go away? Generally, small leaks turn into bigger leaks. For the record, I tried the "hope it will go away" strategy with this problem recently and ended up calling a roofer.
- Have you ever seen a problem employee become a solid performer without intervention? Most likely the answer is no. Generally, the problem employee, at best, remains a small problem. At worst, that person infects others in the organization

or does something that seriously endangers the organization's health or reputation.

- Have you ever had small a problem with a vendor or customer that went unresolved? Perhaps it's a small billing dispute. As time goes on, it compounds until it becomes a bigger issue. Eventually, solving it involves higher levels of management and possibly consultation with legal counsel.

I hope that by now you can see that the logic in dealing with small problems first to keep them from becoming big problems later. Fixing problems early usually requires a relatively small amount of time and energy. It's the difference between putting out a small brush fire and putting out a forest fire.

If you feel as though you are constantly dealing with crisis situations, think about whether decisive action early on may have prevented some of these situations from becoming a crisis in the first place. Occasionally, there are some problems that you can wait out, but most times the problem only gets worse.

I'm not suggesting that anyone ignore big problems, but find a few minutes to step back from the day-to-day problems in your business and consider whether there are some brush fires that you can extinguish quickly and easily before they become forest fires.

▶ *What small problem can you fix today?*

The Ripple Effect

If there is one thing that causes inefficiency in the work place more than any other, it may be ripple effect of missed deadlines. Generally, missed deadlines come in two forms. One is the simple passing of a deadline without its being met. But the other, somewhat more difficult to assess, occurs when a deadline is met with inadequate information or production. Whether we are talking about the flow of internal information or the provision of a product or service to a customer, the result is the same: ultimately, that missed deadline causes a ripple effect throughout the receiving organization and is the cause of substantial inefficiency.

Much like tossing a pebble into a pond, the effect doesn't stop immediately but instead continues almost indefinitely. A missed deadline causes others to spend time waiting, changing their work plan (also known as "scrambling"), and going back to ask people when they will provide what they have already failed to deliver.

Many times, we don't think about the effect of not delivering on a commitment to someone on the other side. While I have never tried to calculate this cost, I have no doubt it is substantial. Perhaps if we could calculate the cost and somehow charge it back when someone didn't deliver as promised, the problem would be solved. While major construction projects many times impose penalties when the final deadline is missed, the same doesn't hold true in most day-to-day activities.

Think of what happens when someone doesn't deliver upon a commitment to you. In the best case, that causes increased pressure on you to do your part in a shorter amount of time and still meet your commitments. In the worst case, the ripple continues to the detriment of companies, departments, and people you may have never thought about or even know about.

Perhaps the worst part of the ripple effect is that it is so difficult to stop once it has started. There is no way to "unthrow" that pebble from the pond. It simply has to run its course. Or, in the business world, someone has to go the extra mile to meet their commitments even though they got a late start. Obviously, the best course is to not let the ripples start. Realizing how big a problem can become, we should all take extra care to not be the pebble in the first place, and that starts with all of us meeting our commitments on a daily basis.

While there are many things that businesses need to do to prepare for the next fiscal year, clarifying expectations around deadlines is certainly one that will add value throughout the year. It gives everyone the chance to be more productive, and that will be appreciated by both your employees and your customers. It might even increase your top line.

▶ *How do missed deadlines impact your organization?*

Simplify

have been working for some time with one of my clients to simplify, and some of the items we are looking at have recently come together. The difference on the administrative side is amazing. We operate with very light staff levels, yet we had someone clamoring for more work. How often do you hear that?

By simply changing our expense reporting, a task that used to take a full day is now accomplished in a few hours. What is the value of freeing six hours of time? Some might argue that it is zero because you can't reduce a full-time employee's salary by six hours and put that money in the bank. Others might take the hourly rate for that employee plus employment taxes, fringe benefits, etc., and multiply by six and argue that this is the value. I would look at it completely differently. Those six hours are extremely valuable. It is like rolling a log down a hill: once you get it going, momentum builds. We used (invested, if you will) those six hours to improve other processes.

Next we tackled our invoicing procedures and, with the help of others in the company, made big improvements. Monthly customer invoicing, which used to take several weeks, is now 95%

complete on the first workday of the month, needing only some minor follow-up to complete the process. Not only did we reduce the hours used to produce invoices, but because they are sent to customers sooner, we get paid sooner, thereby accelerating company cash flow!

These improvements, along with others, released enough hours that we were able to spend a few days resolving a customer issue. We used an administrative resource for a project that otherwise would have been completed by the services delivery staff, who were already over-committed. Although they couldn't find a couple of days to fix the customer issue because of their other priorities, they were thrilled to find a couple of hours to provide oversight and direction. The result was that we resolved an issue that was causing a delay in payments. The customer was delighted, especially because it turned out that the root cause was an error on their part and it was actually their responsibility to fix the issue. Although they knew they should have fixed it, they just didn't have the knowledge or time to get this done. They appreciated that we stepped up and did more than our fair share. They cut checks for the back payments within days of the matter being resolved. The amount of those checks was at least 20 times the hourly rate calculation mentioned previously.

But, of course, it gets better. The hours that we were applying to that ongoing problem were now available to deploy elsewhere. I personally moved two monthly tasks off my plate to others in the organization, now that they weren't as busy. The tasks were necessary, but the procedures were well established and no longer required someone at my level to complete them. I had been doing them only because there wasn't time elsewhere in the organization. Anyone who knows me well knows that I hate doing anything routine more than a couple of times to perfect the process. This freed my time to work on more strategic issues with the CEO.

Whenever you have the opportunity to simplify a process or remove complexity in your organization, I recommend doing so. Not only will you capture the benefits you were anticipating, but you are likely to find hidden benefits as well. The results just might surprise you.

▶ *Start simplifying. You'll be amazed at how quickly the benefits add up.*

Strive For Perfection

Everyone makes mistakes. I used to work with someone who said, "Show me a man who doesn't make mistakes and I'll show you a man who's not doing anything." Probably true, but this is no reason not to strive for perfection. While some mistakes are harmless and can even go unnoticed, others are costly.

If you could take the income statement for a business and capture mistakes just like we capture rent or any other line item, I think you would be surprised by the result. Mistakes have a ripple effect no matter where they start in the organization. Unless they are caught immediately, there may be substantially more work involved in fixing the problem than in performing the original task. Furthermore, the resources required to fix the mistake are usually higher up and are therefore more expensive. If we could calculate the cost of mistakes, we could make thoughtful decisions about how much to spend to address the various underlying issues. Unfortunately, unless you are in a manufacturing environment that tracks rework costs, the vast majority of the expense of fixing mistakes is swept under the rug.

As you think about improving the effectiveness of your organization, think about the sources of mistakes and what you can do to eliminate them. Since it can take hours to fix a mistake that often could have been prevented with a few extra minutes of care, it's almost always worth the time to do some root-cause analysis. Once the cause is understood, then brainstorming some ways to fix the problem is the next step. The following questions are intended to provide some food for thought as you work your way through this process:

- Would a change in procedures help?
- Do the mistakes stem from a particular vendor?
- Does a process need to be better documented?
- Do the people making the mistake know about the problem, or do they need some feedback so that they can be made aware of the problem?
- Is there a mechanical or technological fix that would identify the problem sooner or prevent it from occurring?
- Could someone inspect or review the work before it moves along in the process?
- Might a class or some other form of training help the person doing the work?
- Is a change in staff necessary?

Obviously, this list isn't all-inclusive, but it should stimulate discussion.

I'd encourage every organization to take action to minimize errors in order to improve overall business performance. The time and energy spent fixing errors can certainly be more productively expended growing the business and serving the customer better.

▶ *Are your employees fixing the same mistakes over and over and over again?*

CHAPTER 6

Control The Dollars

Dollars are the lifeblood of a business. The flow of dollars into and out of the business is critical and needs to be both watched and understood.

• Because It Matters

• What Are Your Accounts Receivable Worth?

• Ok To Pay

• Spend It Like It's Your Own

• Don't Go Too Big

• What Is Profit?

• Are You Avoiding Profits?

Because It Matters

Whenever I consult for a new business client, I question every cost that crosses my desk. Why? Because it matters. Every dollar matters, and experience has taught me there is a lot of waste out there. Obviously, I question the big items first, but eventually I question even the small items. A few examples of what I mean by small items are as follows:

An employee was responsible for ordering some logo shirts for the company. She said, "I was talking with another employee and we were wondering if we could use company American Express points and get the shirts without spending any cash." That's a great idea! These two people were thinking like company owners. While the dollars involved are relatively small, their suggestion told senior management that these people both have their heads in the game. Not only did people take notice of their attitude, but their idea earned them each a $50 American Express gift card as well.

Recently, I asked about a $78 monthly invoice. It didn't take long to learn that the cost was supposed to be passed along to a customer two years ago but no one had taken the time to do it. The customer had even agreed! I instructed that the monthly charge be added to the next invoice, and guess what? The customer paid it. No questions asked. Let's think about the math on this one: $78 per month for the last two years is $1,872 that just slipped away. Given that the company was paying the bill, any money received from the customer would fall through to the bottom line. Over a five-year period (the length of the customer contract), this little $78 expense is worth $4,680. While it's not enough money to save the world, these things add up over time, and it was certainly worth the 20 to 30 minutes it took me to find the answer.

I saw a line on a lease invoice for storage space. I asked to see the space and found that it was filled mostly with empty cardboard boxes and a never-used ping pong table. I checked the lease document and found that it was on a month-to-month basis. And this wasn't some $50 per month lease at a public storage facility; this was $577 per month in a downtown building! If you have been paying attention, I'm sure you can guess what I did next. I talked to the person responsible for storage and explained that the annual cost came to $6,924. At the same time, the staff in this department had just asked to spend $7,000 for new computer equipment. Interesting how those numbers almost match.

If you think these examples of small mistakes are interesting, you should ask me about the bigger ones sometime. Some people think that questioning expenditures is the job of the finance manager alone. But I think it is the job of everyone who touches the process of spending money.

▶ *Ask! It matters!*

What Are Your Accounts Receivable Worth?

Almost every business has Accounts Receivable (AR) that are older than they would like. Managing them can be a difficult process. To start, management has to be honest with themselves about the value of their AR.

Too frequently, management allows old AR to sit on the books and ignores the problem. Often, they don't want to take the write-down and absorb the loss into their financial statements. Obviously, these old AR will lower current earnings as well as negatively affect their debt/equity ratio, and they are concerned about the impact this might have when they show their financial statements to the bank. I've got news for companies that take this approach. The bank is making those adjustments in any event. They always wipe out old AR on the assumption that they are uncollectable. Not only is management getting dinged for the old AR, but at the same time they are also taking a subtle knock from their banker for not recognizing this on their own and then taking an allowance for doubtful accounts.

One of my clients had two particular customers, each with substantial AR balances of about $50,000. We applied the same process to each customer and the results from the two customers are likely going to end up being the exact opposite of each other. In both cases, the balance built up over some time even though payments were being made. (Sometimes they paid an amount lower than the monthly service, and sometimes they missed the monthly payment entirely, with a promise to make good "soon.") At some point, however, both customers got a shut-off notice.

The first customer made a substantial payment upon receiving the notice and then made payments each month that covered current services as well as some payment against the amount past due. It took some time, but eventually they owed only about $700, and that was all within terms. In the end, this scenario worked out well for all parties. We got paid in full and have a very loyal customer because we helped them work through a challenging time in their business.

The second customer story isn't nearly as good. It starts out the same, but by the time we sent our shut-off notice the IRS was taking action. As a general rule, the IRS is the 3,000-pound gorilla in the room and almost always wins. Now we're part of a creditor group and there is no telling how much of the remaining balance we'll recover from the dollars (if any) left after the IRS debt is settled. Ultimately, the customer is out of business. Had we moved sooner, our exposure likely would have been smaller, and the customer probably would have failed sooner.

Recently, I had lunch with a great business attorney. Her advice was that every company should have a defined process of taking a certain action at 30 days past due, at 60, at 90, and eventually turning the account over to an attorney or collection agency. Good advice.

The message is that every business should realistically review its Accounts Receivable on a regular basis. No one is well served by leaving doubtful AR on the books and hoping they will someday turn good. I've never regretted calling a customer early about an outstanding balance. But there certainly have been times that I've regretted waiting.

▶ *What are your Accounts Receivable really worth?*

OK To Pay

The normal process of approving accounts payable is for someone who actually received the goods or services to indicate that the invoice is correct and the goods or services were appropriately received. Often, this is indicated by the phrase "OK to Pay" or simply "OK" written on the invoice. But what do these words really mean? I've come to learn that it really depends upon whose initials appear beneath the phrase.

In some cases it means, "I have reviewed this invoice, it is accurate in terms of what we agreed to pay, the goods or services have been received and are of good quality, and as a responsible member of the company I approve payment." Of course, none of those other words are actually written on the invoice—they are just implied. When an invoice like this crosses my desk, it is almost always paid within terms.

In other cases, OK means, "I am scribbling my name at the bottom of this invoice to get it off my desk." Just as in the first case, those words aren't on the page either, but trust me, they are very much part of the message. These invoices almost always get challenged, delaying the payment process.

The trick for the finance professional is to know who is providing them with the first answer and who is providing the second. If you are part of the payment chain, from the CFO to the accounts payable staff, it's your job to figure this out.

Let me give you two examples that actually landed on my desk. The first was lease termination paperwork that offered a buyout price of $5,900. I challenged this number, and after leaving just one voice mail message, I got a reply message indicating that the lessee could agree do the buyout at $4,728. This saved my client $1,172. In another case, we were closing out a maintenance contract and being billed for a 30-day notification period. There were some extenuating circumstances, so I asked the person who had indicated that the invoice was "OK to Pay" if he had challenged it. It was pretty clear that he had not. Again, a quick phone call to the vendor resulted in the 30-day notification period being waived, saving $1,443.

The point of these two examples isn't to toot my own horn but to provide a good illustration how just being on the ball can translate into significant savings for the company.

If you're part of the finance group, learn who is diligent about approving invoices and who is just going through the motions. And if you're one of those people responsible for approving invoices, spend a few minutes thinking about the invoice before you initial it for payment. You might be the one able to save your company money.

▶ *What does "OK to Pay" mean to you?*

Spend It Like It's Your Own

Everyone should spend company money like it's their own. I constantly come across situations in which employees are spending company money very much unlike it was their own.

While there are some people who treat company funds as if they were their own—and you should value these employees—there are also those who don't give much thought to how they spend the company's money. The general attitude is: "it's not my money." This is so common that there is a well-recognized term for it in corporate circles: Other People's Money (OPM).

While the extreme example of this attitude is Dennis Kozlowski of Tyco International, who spent company money lavishly on himself (remember the $6,000 shower curtain?) and those close to him, most companies have small examples of spending that could be better managed.

More commonplace examples of this are:

- Company meals that are more frequent or more expensive than necessary

- Travel accommodations that don't consider reasonable or cost-effective alternatives
- Cell phones or Internet plans that might be less expensive, if only someone were to ask
- Expense requests without reasonable alternatives or multiple bids
- Company credit cards that go unchecked

Now at this point you are probably thinking that I am going to suggest a myriad of controls to prevent overspending. Quite the contrary. I am not a big fan of policies and procedures.

Years ago, a company for which I worked issued a new travel policy. It was so complicated that many, myself included, didn't bother to read or apprehend it. When my boss asked me to explain it to him, I told him that the word within the company was that it was so hard to understand that virtually no one had read it. He said to me, "But you just took a trip! How did you book your tickets?" My reply was, "I booked the tickets that I would have booked if I was paying for the trip myself." He thought for a moment and said, "Thanks, that's what I'll do."

Rather than suggesting that you implement policies and procedures, I'd like to convince everyone that the best and simplest approach is for employees to act as if they are spending their own money. Because, in effect, they are. Face it, there is only so much money to go around, and money that is wasted in one area isn't available to grow the business, provide employee raises, or make necessary capital improvements. Obviously, getting employees to understand this is easier said than done, but it is not impossible.

▶ *Do your employees spend company money like it's their own?*

Don't Go Too Big

The saying during the dot-com boom was go big or go home. It meant that anything worth doing was worth doing in a big way. Hence, many of the start-up companies of the day had world domination on the mind and were spending huge amounts of cash to invest in growth.

Ironically, that very philosophy was part of the reason that many of these companies failed. While it's smart to plan for growth, there is a huge difference between planning for potential upside and acting as if it that upside is a certainty. In the first case, the thought process is, "How will we respond if volume doubles or triples during the next 12 months? How will we staff, obtain additional office space, meet customer demand, and so forth?" Generally, that's a smart way to think, and it should be accompanied by some downside thinking as well.

On the other hand, when one assumes that growth is a certainty, then the attitude tends to be, "Let's just buy it now because we're going to need it someday anyway." The spending associated with that thinking can (and has) crashed companies. While this phenomenon was typical of the dot-com days, it can still be seen today when companies are focused exclusively on growth to the exclusion of day-to-day operations and current positive cash flow.

There are costs associated with planning for growth that doesn't occur. The costs show as overinflated rents owing to too much space and excessive build-out costs; software systems that can support substantial growth but are excessive for current operations; employee benefits packages that are not "market" for the company's size; uncontrolled spending of "future" profits; and myriad other costs.

While planning for growth is an important step for any business, assuming growth and needlessly committing to costs substantially in excess of those required to support near-term business can be devastating. It can starve the company of resources required for current operations. The company is then forced to either do without or face the option of taking on additional debt or equity (dilutive of current shareholders) to fund those costs.

The best way to avoid this trap is to plan spending on the basis of milestones or accomplishments. Linking spending to milestones that measure success, particularly marketplace success, is an approach that will assure you and the investors that there is a reason to be optimistic about the future. Putting these milestones in writing will force you to measure actual results against expectations and therefore force a realistic assessment of the business compared to those expectations.

While I recognize that this approach is less exciting than the approach that assumes big growth and therefore big spending, it's far more likely to keep you and your company in the game much longer.

As most of the dot-com companies learned, when they went far too big the result was that they indeed "went home."

▶ *Remember, if you go too big, you will likely go home.*

What Is Profit?

The amount earned on the capital deployed in the business is considered profit. One of the more common measurements of the efficiency of capital deployment is Return on Investment (ROI), although there are certainly other measurements.

But to measure ROI, you first have to get the profit number on the income statement right. Too often, financial statements fail to capture all the costs of running a business so you cannot discern from the income statement the true profit of the business.

In big companies, the profit picture can be skewed by transfer prices between divisions as well as by overhead allocations from corporate. The staffs of large companies have spent countless hours arguing over these and other issues that can drastically affect the profit of operating divisions.

In smaller companies, the issues are different but the result is the same—an income statement that doesn't accurately portray the profit picture of the business. Profit can be misstated for many reasons, but here are a few that tend to be commonplace:

- *Owners provide "free" labor.* It is common for a business owner to record his or her salary at a below-market rate. In effect, he or she is contributing labor that makes the profitability of the business appear better than it should.

- *Interest free loans.* Owners sometimes lend their company money at below-market rates or at no interest at all. This results in an inflated profit number. A similar phenomenon occurs with rent when the owner of the business also owns the building.

- *Failure to capture depreciation.* Machinery wears out and must be replaced. The estimated cost of this expense should be captured monthly.

- *Supplier invoices not posted in a timely manner.* The result can be a shifting of profits from one period (month, quarter) to the next.

- *No allowance for bad debt.* Most businesses have receivables that they can't collect, but I've seen businesses carry these on the books at full value when the likelihood of collecting them is slim.

The main point to remember is that by not capturing all the relevant costs of running a business, owners can't know the true profit nor can they know the return on the capital they have invested in the business. Aren't both worth knowing?

▶ *What's your profit?*

Are You Avoiding Profits?

Most under-performing businesses don't suffer from a lack of market demand, intense competition, or other external factors. Rather, they suffer from a lack of accountability within the organization. I believe that accountability causes profits, and lack of accountability can most assuredly cause a lack of profits.

While it might not always be true that an accountable organization will be a profitable organization, I would argue that a lack of accountability will certainly cause a lack of profits. And by that I mean that the organization will actually be losing money or at least could be making much more.

Just as Einstein discovered E=mc2, I have discovered that *a lack of accountability will cause a lack of profits*. While I realize that a comparison to Einstein is a somewhat bold and outrageous statement, surely there is sufficient anecdotal evidence in most businesses to see what happens when people aren't held accountable. Generally, everyone suffers—employees, stockholders, suppliers, and customers.

While some of those constituencies might feel as though they are held hostage to the lack of accountability, it's rare that they don't have the ability to go somewhere else. Employees can find another job, stockholders can sell their shares or choose not to invest more resources, suppliers can charge extra for the difficulty they have dealing with an unaccountable organization, and customers most certainly will choose to spend their money elsewhere. Given sufficient time, all of them will eventually make another choice.

What causes the lack of accountability? Often it is a desire to avoid dealing with conflict. I believe, however, that conflict, at least constructive conflict, is good. It forces people to clarify their beliefs, expectations, positions, and views about how everyone in the organization fulfills their roles and responsibilities and how the organization serves customers.

If a sales person isn't achieving the set goals, then that is a point of discussion. If the accounting department isn't delivering accurate reports on time, then someone needs to address the issue. If the phones aren't being answered appropriately, then someone must speak to the receptionist. Too often, people would rather avoid the issue than raise it and have an uncomfortable conversations by holding someone accountable.

If you're avoiding the conflict that comes with accountability, then you're avoiding profits.

▶ *Are you avoiding profits?*

CHAPTER 7

Driving For Results

For anything to get done, someone has to be the driving force. Who sets the tone in your organization?

• Set The Agenda

• Who's The "Push"?

• Push Back

• To Whom Are You Accountable?

• What's Your Deadline?

Set The Agenda

If you don't set the agenda, one will be set for you. Guaranteed. Even if you do take the initiative and set an agenda, there is some chance that the boss will overrule you on some or even all of it. But at least you have taken a shot. Whether you're in finance or another discipline, it's important to walk in with a plan. To do otherwise is to let the thoughts of others or the events of the day control you—not a good idea.

Instead, take a few moments, or as long as necessary, to set the agenda. Before you start your day or walk into a meeting, make a plan. Doing so will show initiative and forethought. Ultimately, those are qualities that people are looking for in leaders.

Think about how a meeting might turn out differently under these two scenarios.

Scenario 1: You walk into a meeting to discuss your plan for the week, month, year, or project—except that you have no plan. The next thing you know, the boss is throwing ideas your way. Some are good, and some are not so good. Or worse, some are bad, and some are really bad.

At this point, you're stuck. You either accept those ideas or you end up arguing about them or negotiating their execution. In either event, you've lost the opportunity to influence control over your work and your time.

Scenario 2: You walk into the same meeting with your own agenda. You have a plan, and the boss sees that you took the time to think about business needs and priorities. Whether the boss agrees with all your ideas or not, you're likely to walk out with 80% of your plan in place. In fact, if the boss is busy, he or she might leave it alone if the only disagreement concerns small parts of it. The boss will move on to things that have a higher priority, and you'll end up with your plan accepted in its entirety. And even if the boss disagrees with most of it and makes substantial changes, they'll likely respect the fact that you cared enough to present your thoughts.

Always come forward with your agenda. In the best case, it gives you a chance to exercise greater control and take action based upon what you think is in the best interest of the company. In the worst case, it lets those above you and around you know that you are acting like a leader. Think about it. What do you want from your employees? Someone to come into your office and ask, "Boss, what should I do?" Or to have them come in and say, "Here's my plan." The answer is obvious.

▶ *Never miss an opportunity to set the agenda.*

Who's The "Push"?

When I was 15 years old, I worked the summer splitting my time between two contractors. (I guess I was employing the fractional concept even then.) To this day, I remember some of the lessons learned on those jobs. Some of those lessons have served me well living in an older home, but more of them have served me well in dealing with people and business issues.

I remember being called aside by the boss one day when he was leaving and told that I needed to be the Push while he was gone. "What's the Push?" was my obvious question. He explained to me that on any job, the Push is the one person responsible for setting the tone and pushing people to get things accomplished.

People tend to excel when challenged to do more. While some naturally push themselves to accomplish as much as possible, others need an external push to do their best. I tend to be competitive by nature, and I know that I work better with a team of equally motivated individuals.

Years later, as I look at small businesses that are languishing, I see that the problem with many is that they have no Push. No one is setting the tone or holding people within the organization accountable for goals and objectives. Usually, someone filled this role at one point. But as time has gone by, that person has either left the organization or lost their enthusiasm for the business. The result is an organization that lacks drive.

Employees show up, perform their tasks in a routine manner, and walk out the door at the end of the day. Sometimes it's a problem with the rewards system or the lack of one; at other times it's a problem with a few rotten apples; and at still others it is the example set at the top. But whatever the cause of the problem, the results show up on the financial statements.

So, the next time that you sit down and look at your financial statements (why not do it today?), ask yourself if you're getting all that you can from your business.

If you have a business with no Push, then you have a business that is not achieving its revenue potential and has too much cost in the system. If you wonder why you're not generating the cash flow that you think you should or that you once did in the past, then perhaps you need to ask:

▶ *"Who's the Push?"*

Push Back

It is important to strongly advocate your position. I don't suggest arguing just to be argumentative (we all know people who do that). Rather, be a strong advocate for your position and beliefs. This was brought home to me recently when a service provider sent one of my clients a bill for an extra $2,600. Although the amount is small, it still serves to make a valuable point.

They had proposed a fixed price, but there is no doubt in my mind that they did extra work. On the other hand, they were beginning to develop a pattern of asking for "a few more dollars." Still, their request wasn't unreasonable. Moreover, there was a relationship to protect. I shot back a quick email pointing out that they had come back too many times with these types of requests. I reminded them that this had been a fixed bid and that I had discussed with them the possibility of moving the account early on. I offered to split the difference with them. That was the fair solution under this set of circumstances. They quickly accepted that offer and the issue was resolved.

I don't blame them for asking. Unforeseen things happen all the time, and it requires both sides to be flexible if they want to maintain a long-term relationship.

But that is not the real point of the story. The real question is what they truly thought about the email they received. I think the real answer came several weeks later when they sent another email my way asking if I'd be interested in an introduction that might result in more business on my end. Simply put, the action that I'd taken helped to earn their respect.

Whenever you make an introduction, you are putting your reputation on the line. Clearly, they respected our position on this relatively small billing dispute as well as the way in which we handled it. Otherwise, they wouldn't be willing to risk their reputation by suggesting the referral. There is never anything wrong with strongly advocating your position. My experience is that 99% of the time the other side is going to respect you for standing up for yourself, your client, or your company. That's what business is about.

Of course, I offer one caveat. My newsletter is emailed to more than 30,000 people across the United States and internationally. Cultures differ. They differ geographically and from company to company. One has to be sensitive to these differences. The style that worked for me when I worked on the East Coast doesn't play nearly as well in the Midwest, where people tend to be much less confrontational. My first job was at Unisys, where you could have a heated argument during the day and no one gave it a second thought by the time they got to the employees' usual watering hole.

Adapt your style to fit the situation. For most people, this is easier said than done. But if you don't adapt, you will likely not win your case, and you won't be respected, either.

▶ *Don't accept every bill that comes in the door. If the circumstances warrant, push back.*

To Whom Are You Accountable?

One of the trickier problems for small businesses is accountability of the boss. Whether it is a sole proprietor, family-owned business, or one that is majority controlled with silent minority partners, accountability is often a real problem. I've found that organizations in which there is a strong measure of accountability perform better than those in which accountability is weak.

While it might sound great to some to operate in an environment in which they are not held accountable to a higher authority, the truth is that accountability drives results. It is easy to allow things to slide or not be as driven as you should when no one is looking over your shoulder. It happens to all but the most driven of us.

I've worked as an employee and a consultant for both kinds of organizations. Ultimately, I would much rather deal with the stresses of accountability than work with businesses that come without it, because these are organizations that underperform.

In all organizations, it's necessary for the leaders to hold their direct reports accountable, for them to hold the next level down accountable, and so on down the line. The problem in an organization in which the top person isn't accountable is that it starts to set a precedent. That person doesn't feel the pressure of accountability to a higher authority, and over time this lack of accountability can creep into the organization. Sooner or later, you have an organization where people are showing up but aren't necessarily driven to improve performance day in and day out. Remember, only 33.33% of life is just showing up.

So, what should business owners or managers do if no one is holding them accountable? They need to *create* accountability. While this can be as formal as having a board of directors, it can be as informal as finding trusted advisors or mentors who can provide a level of accountability on a monthly or quarterly basis.

One of the roles that I typically play for my clients is to be this accountability supervisor in organizations. I either do this directly or by ensuring that there is regular reporting and transparency to the board or other stakeholders.

If you are serious about improving your business, I'd suggest that you create an accountability framework for yourself. If you're not ready to reach out to others, create a list of *must do* items (not should, want, or hope to do but *must* do) and hold yourself accountable for the results. I'd be surprised if you don't see an improvement in your business performance after the first quarter. From there, things should only get better.

▶ *How can you create more accountability in your business?*

What's Your Deadline?

That's a question that comes up a lot, and people may or may not give much thought to the answer. My wife asked me that question about a project that I was working on recently, and it actually caught me by surprise. I had been working on the project as time allowed and hadn't made it a real priority. Consequently, progress has been slow, as projects with committed deadlines (almost all of them) consumed my time and resources and got done first.

During the *60 Minutes* interview of Walter Isaacson, who wrote what will likely be the authoritative biography of Steve Jobs, Isaacson said the Jobs would put forward deadlines that everyone around him thought impossible, and that it was through Jobs' sheer force of will and insistence on meeting the deadline that the goal would actually be met. That's a powerful thought. The action of choosing a deadline can be so motivating that it makes the seemingly impossible occur.

I remember my very first corporate job. There was a project list, and in one of the columns was the word *deadline*. In the very next column were the words *revised deadline*. How many times do you think the original deadline was met? Almost never. By incorporating a revised deadline into the report, the powers that be had acknowledged that they expected the deadline to be missed. No one took the original deadline seriously.

These diverse examples about the power of deadlines demonstrate that they are more important than most people realize. When a deadline is set, that is an opportunity to send a message about the importance of the project and about management's expectations. That message can be either motivating or demotivating. Are deadlines an imperative in your organization? Do people go to extraordinary measures to meet them? Or, as the old joke goes, is it more like: "I love deadlines, especially the whooshing sound they make as they go flying by?"

The deadline culture can make a huge difference in your organization's performance. I've worked in many places, from those where deadlines were essentially ignored to those where they were considered an imperative and people worked extraordinarily hard to meet them. It is without question that an organization that respects deadlines gets more done and performs at a higher standard than those that take a more relaxed approach.

None of this should be construed as my saying that a deadline should be arbitrary and capricious. Setting deadlines that don't consider the magnitude of the work and the people responsible for doing it will most likely be ignored. But, that said, using aggressive deadlines that challenge people (even if those deadlines are initially thought to be unrealistic) will get more out of the organization than most thought possible. Moreover, doing this will leave everyone in the organization feeling good about themselves. They will recognize that they achieved something they didn't think possible and that their boundaries are far beyond what they previously believed.

▶ *The next time you begin a project, ask:* ***what's your deadline?***

CHAPTER 8

It's Uncertain Out There: Plan for It

No plan can account for every possibility. But the point of developing a financial plan isn't to account for every conceivable possibility but to consider the most likely ones and then to develop a set of contingency plans that one can turn to when things don't go as planned (which is almost all the time).

• Risk

• Planning In Volatile Times

• Plan For The Unexpected

• How's The Economy?

• Sustainable Growth

• Time Your Exit

Risk

All businesses take some amount of risk. Just opening the doors for the first time involves the risk of capital and labor. From then on, every business decision could be thought of as a risk-reward trade-off. We probably don't take the time to think of most decisions in that light. We go about our day-to-day activities and accept the risks in our business. But there are certain decisions for which one should definitely be thinking about risk and how it affects the overall business.

I believe that many businesses become more risky over time. While most small businesses don't specifically measure investment activities versus their risk-adjusted cost of capital, larger businesses, certainly the Fortune 500, do so regularly. But even these businesses are not necessarily good at it. Too often, they tend to assume that all the projects they undertake have the same risk profile.

For the moment, let's assume that there are only three risk categories (high, medium, and low) and that the business operates in the middle (medium). Let's also assume that a fair return on those projects is 20% for high-risk projects, 15% for medium-risk, and 10% for low-risk. The specific numbers in this case are for illustration and not meant to suggest that they are the correct return ratios for any particular business.

Over time, a business will look at many investment opportunities. If they measure all of them against a medium (15%) investment threshold without considering individual project risk, the result will be a shifting of risk over time. Low-risk projects won't meet the medium-risk threshold and will get denied (even though you shouldn't expect them to achieve as high a return because they are safer). The high-risk projects will disproportionally exceed the return threshold because they aren't being held to a high enough standard. More of these projects will get approved, and a higher than anticipated amount will fail. The ultimate result will likely be a business whose risk profile shifts over time.

Think about what has happened in the financial services markets lately. There is a strong argument to be made that there was a lack of understanding of the risk of the underlying investments. Simply put, historical mortgage default rates (and therefore risk) of people who used traditional mortgages with 20% down payments is lower than that of highly leveraged "nothing down" borrowers. Clearly, the underwriting assumptions were not sufficiently risk adjusted as their roots were likely based upon the former group but underpinned investments in the latter. The result was a mismatch of the risk-return paradigm.

So, how does a small business deal with assessing risk? To start, I would suggest thinking about the risk profile of individual project decisions and ask some questions. Are the assumptions conservative or aggressive? Have we completed a similar project before? What is our confidence that we can achieve the result? Can we accurately measure the results? How have others fared in similar circumstances?

If you conclude that a project is high risk, make sure that you are getting adequately compensated for that risk. On the other hand, if the investment opportunity is low risk, it should not be ignored just because it doesn't meet a preset threshold that doesn't consider that fact.

▶ *Can you distinguish high risk endeavors from ones that are low risk?*

Planning In Volatile Times

There is an old saying: when opportunity knocks, answer the door. But when times are volatile, it is hard to know whether or not you are looking at an opportunity. You could get whiplash just watching the stock market, with prices up or down 10% in a single day. Take your eye off the ball for even a short period of time and the environment in which you are operating can be different from what it was when you last looked.

During one of my first corporate jobs, I wondered again and again why the treasurer waited to make decisions. As I got to know both him and the company, I learned that it wasn't procrastination, but keeping options open. At the time, we had some relatively straightforward financing decisions. It was common practice for us not to commit until the last possible moment. There was a lot of merit to that practice, and over the years it added substantial value to the company. I routinely wonder if those decision makers still operate in the same manner or if they are more decisive in their actions. Today, what seems like an opportunity one moment can appear to be an expensive proposition the next.

There is always an opportunity to capitalize on short-term market fluctuations. But the key is recognizing that fluctuations—in some cases, bubbles—are short term. People have short memories. In 1999 and early 2000, we thought that Internet stocks would increase forever (and I certainly wish I had sold at the first sign of a downturn). A few years ago, many people thought they should buy the biggest house possible (with the smallest possible down payment) because "everyone knew" housing prices would keep going up at 20% a year and that this was an easy way to make money. More recently, we had predictions by "the experts" that gas and oil prices would continue to soar after hitting $4.00 per gallon at the pump. After pushing nearly $150 per barrel just a few months ago, oil prices are under $70 per barrel as I am writing this (October 2008). As I get ready to publish this book (2013) oil is just under $100 per barrel and while we don't know where the price will be next year, we can be certain that we'll see constant price changes along the way.

The lesson to be learned here is that nothing lasts forever. It can't. The laws of economics dictate that behaviors will change. Those who take advantage of short-term market opportunities profit. Those who react to them after the fact will lose. Those who sit tight and place long-term bets will likely be okay in the long run, but it will be a rollercoaster ride along the way.

With that in mind, unless your business is taking advantage of a window of opportunity, business decision making should be long-term focused. It's certainly advisable to take advantage of short-term opportunities, but it's crucial they are recognized as just that.

▶ *Extrapolating short-term trends into the distant future is often a mistake. Don't react. Plan.*

Plan For The Unexpected

Earlier, I posed the following question: *it's mid-year, are you in control?*

For those that live in Saint Louis, Missouri, that proved to be an even more interesting question than I originally thought. In July a few years ago, I advised in my monthly newsletter that mid-year was a good time for businesses to examine whether they were in control of costs. Not long after, a series of severe storms hit the area and nearly half a million homes and businesses lost power, some for as long as a week. Businesses, both large and small, had to react. Or did they?

Some businesses have disaster recovery plans in place with details on how to handle such situations. Others have at least thought about it and have some ideas about how to react. And still others are caught totally off-guard.

Obviously, the impact of the storms and power outages affected everyone differently. The owner of a tree service told me it was an opportunity to provide around-the-clock services to both old and new customers. An insurance executive told me that despite having disaster recovery plans in place, the implementation wasn't smooth and customers could not reach the company (and this was during a time when customers felt they most needed to reach their insurer the most). An Internet Service Provider told me that they are prepared for events like this with redundant power and bandwidth in their data centers.

By now, you might be wondering the point of this. It's that businesses should plan for both normal events and for the unexpected. Think about the five or ten events that could affect your business and plan. While I'm not suggesting that every business needs a complete disaster recovery plan, most could benefit from a half-day session of talking about events that are outside the norm and how you might handle them when they occur. Then, when something unusual happens, you'll have given enough thought to various possibilities and be able to take action. While I stress the need for planning in your business, let us never forget that all the planning in the world is useless if it's not followed by action. That being said, a plan is still a great way to start.

▶ *Have you planned for the unexpected?*

How's The Economy?

People frequently ask me, "How's the economy?" They do this because I work with multiple companies and have insights into their performance against plan and the prior year. But the truth is that I don't spend many cycles thinking about the overall economy.

While I believe that it's necessary to be conscious of the current economic climate in which you are operating, this is also a bit like understanding the weather forecast. You can and should prepare for it, but there is nothing you can do to change it.

Most companies are built (at least in the near term) around an expectation of a certain business volume for the upcoming year. I have seen companies blow the doors off their plan in a bad economy, and I've seen companies struggle when the economy is on a roll. Although it's important to understand the economic environment in which you operate, I believe that the performance of most businesses is guided more by their internal operations, marketing, customer service, and so forth, than it is by the overall economy.

The US economy is $14 trillion annually. Even the largest businesses are merely trying to get a very small share of the pie. And even if the whole pie is shrinking (as in a recession) the easy answer is just to steal a piece of someone else's pie (market share). Easier said than done, for sure, but the truth is that companies are battling for market share all the time, and every company needs to be doing its absolute best to attract market share regardless of the economy.

Too many companies blame the economy for the lack of business without asking themselves if they are doing everything possible to maximize business in the environment in which they are operating.

In some cases, a bad economy might mean hunkering down and watching costs to survive the economic storm, but I tend to favor a contrarian approach. If you have prepared for a rainy day, I think it is far better to spend extra resources to gather business during bad times. Slow economic environments tend to shake out the weaker players in any industry or marketplace.

This is why it is so important for businesses to have a reserve. Too many small businesses distribute nearly every available dollar to the owners during good times. Doing this wouldn't be that bad if the owners kept some funds aside, knowing that they might have to put it back into the business during slow times, but as often as not this money is tied up in illiquid investments or simply consumed. This leaves a business with little staying power when things slow down, and these are the companies that don't survive.

Understand the economy. Plan for bad times, because they will certainly occur from time to time. But do everything in your power to maximize your business despite the economy. Take advantage of this fact and aggressively go after the competition. When things get better, you will be that much stronger for it.

▶ *You have to operate in both good economics and bad.*

Sustainable Growth

Some time ago, I worked with a formula called the sustainable growth rate model. Generally, it takes a company's profit margins, the amount it wishes to retain for growth (as opposed to the amount it will pay out as compensation to management or dividends to investors) and compares this amount to the projected net assets required to support growth. It also factors in the company's leverage ratio—how much it finances through debt versus equity.

For those of you who haven't thought in mathematical equations since being tested on them at the end of the semester (myself included), let me try to put that in plain English. Generally, the after-tax profit margin minus dividends paid out to shareholders leaves capital available for growth. Every dollar of growth requires so much capital to support it. Depending upon the life cycle of the company, this may be made up of funds for working capital (accounts receivable, for example), or it may be capital expenditures for capacity expansion.

Whatever the specific makeup, the point is that there is a certain amount of growth a company can support based upon internally generated funds. Furthermore, most companies operate with a certain ratio of debt and equity. As a company grows, it can generally support more debt. Growth beyond that must be supported by additional outside capital, either by issuing new equity or increasing the leverage of the firm. Whether the company chooses to fund expansion with debt or equity will determine the amount of leverage and therefore the financing risk that the business takes on.

Obviously, just because a formula determines a growth rate doesn't mean a company can actually grow at that rate. Market and competitive factors as well as the company's management team are critical factors. The formula is simply meant to suggest the maximum rate at which the company can grow given certain financial assumptions.

The rate at which a company grows and how it chooses to finance its growth, however, are issues that every company must deal with one way or another. They may choose to grow with internally generated capital, to issue new equity, to borrow to fund growth, or ultimately not to grow beyond their comfort zone. Some companies spend time thinking about these issues during their strategic planning process. Others may simply operate within their comfort zone, and that itself is an implicit decision about leverage, growth, and risk tolerance guided by the ownership/ management group.

If you believe you have growth opportunities ahead of you, it's worth spending some time working through various growth assumptions and how those might be financed over both the short and long term.

▶ *How fast can you grow?*

Time Your Exit

Companies are sold for a variety of reasons. The driving issue can be strategic fit, capital needs, succession planning (especially in the case of family-held businesses), duration (in the case of private equity firms), or other factors.

Regardless of the reason, for businesses that have reached some level of maturity (i.e., other than high-growth businesses that need capital to grow the company), the best way to maximize value is to be in a position where you do not have to sell. When a company is forced to sell, in many cases they have few alternatives and will be lucky to find one potential buyer—that is, if they can get a deal done at all. In these situations, the golden rule prevails: he who has the gold rules. The seller is likely to end up with a take-it-or-leave-it offer and, with no other choices, will likely take it.

On the other hand, when a company is strong there may be multiple potential buyers. Some may see a strategic fit and some may see substantial operating synergies, while some others may be purely financial buyers seeking to acquire the company for its strong operating cash flows. In cases such as these, a seller will likely be able to generate interest from a handful of potential buyers and create a bidding war for the company. The result will be a much higher transaction price than what could be obtained in the absence of competition.

So, how does a business achieve such an enviable position, where multiple potential buyers are clamoring for the same business? The answer is that the company must build a business that has real value. That may be intellectual property, strong distribution, a particularly strong product line-up, real or perceived barriers to entry, or strong Earnings Before Interest, Taxes, Depreciation and Amortization (EBITDA) and cash flow. Most likely, the business has more than one of these characteristics. And when companies have one or more key value propositions, they have options when it comes to exit timing.

Too often, businesses, especially small businesses, are looking to sell at a time when they are weak. For one reason or another (usually cash flow or lack thereof), they have to sell. I have literally sat across the table from sellers like this, and while they try to argue for higher value, astute buyers know that they are the ones in control. They will put just enough on the table to get a deal done and not a penny more.

Some will argue that the sale of a business is something that should be planned three to five years in advance. If you are running a business that doesn't have one or more of the value propositions mentioned previously, then that is certainly true. You will need time to develop value in the business. If, on the other hand, the business has been run from Day 1 with an eye toward value creation, then I would argue that the business is always in shape for a transaction.

Run your business in a way that creates lasting value. That puts you in control when the time comes to sell your business, whether you initiate the sale or the opportunity of a lifetime comes your way.

▶ *A business of lasting value gives you options. And options are always valuable.*

CHAPTER 9

Are You Dealing With The Facts?

Too many business decisions are made without facts. In some situations, I have cried out for even a "factoid" (which is not a whole fact, just a piece of one). Businesses need facts not only to make good decisions but to take the emotion out of the decision.

• Assess The Situation

• Be Accountable To The Facts

• Let The Numbers Be Your Guide

• A Clerical Error Causes Bankruptcy

• Juggling Cash

• Questions

• Mark It On Your Calendar

Assess The Situation

I am all for action. Frankly, my bias is toward digging in and starting work rather than developing a detailed action plan of what needs to be done. That being said, in solving any problem you need a general direction of where you are going and the facts about any problem that you are trying to solve.

Some years ago, I saw a technology executive in action during several moments of crisis. When all of those around him were scurrying about, he would retreat to his office for some peace and quiet. At first, it appeared that he wasn't engaged. But quite the opposite was true. He was trying to assess the situation before taking action. Generally, he went through the process of trying to determine: what do we know? What don't we know? What do we need to know? What facts are available to us that we don't yet have? What won't we be able to know no matter how much time we spend trying to find out?

It was with this background that he would develop several theories about what was wrong and what actions he could take to get more information that would help him to better understand the problem. It was from this basis that he started to work on solutions.

By comparison, others around him were making assumptions about the cause of the problem and proposing solutions based upon those assumptions. Commonly the actions they took did nothing to solve the problem and only caused a delay as their "solutions" were implemented. When they failed to solve the problem, it was back to the drawing board—or in this case, guessing board. The end result was that it took longer to solve the problem than it should have.

Whenever you're dealing with a problem, it's critical to get a handle on the facts. While it might be uncomfortable to stop and assess the problem in the midst of a crisis, it is far more efficient than trying solutions that may or may not be appropriate under the circumstances. That way, you can be sure that your actions are appropriate and are improving the situation—not just providing action for action's sake.

▶ *Gather the facts so you can assess before you act.*

Be Accountable To The Facts

While there are some who thrive on conflict, I think it's fair to say that most people prefer to avoid it. However, business conflict doesn't have to be confrontational, disagreeable, or argumentative if people start with the facts. That is why solid reporting of business results—both financial and non-financial measures—is critical to the health of the organization.

Rather than discussing opposing points of view and arguing over vague and possibly accusatory statements, a much more rational discussion is possible if both parties have the facts and are literally looking at the same sheet of paper. Let's look at a few examples.

> An employee tends to show up late and leave early while still clocking 40 hours. Rather than confront the employee with a statement such as, "You're always late," present them with actual hours for a week and ask them why they should be paid for time they didn't work. Most likely, they'll agree with you.

A customer recently questioned whether a vendor could handle the business. The customer feared that the vendor would be swamped because they had a lot of product to ship. Upon further probing, the vendor learned that the order wouldn't even amount to half a truckload per week (whereas they consider a truckload per day a big customer).

Customer service staff report that everything is "under control," yet the facts show that customers are on hold for nearly an hour. If there were a proper reporting of call statistics, there would be no debate.

I talk to many companies about their performance. It's amazing how few times someone can speak using numbers and percentages. Rather, I hear, "We're doing great," or worse, "OK," which means they probably don't know how they are really doing.

Recently I attended the annual military skills competition at the United States Military Academy at West Point. Arguably, this is the most accountable place on the face of the earth. I have made this trip several times and it serves as a reminder of what accountability really means. Many businesses could learn lessons of accountability from West Point.

▶ *To avoid conflict, don't avoid the issue. Just talk numbers. You'll take both the emotion and the conflict out of the discussion.*

Let The Numbers Be Your Guide

Business is based upon facts. Or at least it should be. Anecdotal evidence is fine for adding some color commentary and improving the depth of understanding, but it is no substitute for dealing with the cold, hard facts.

I started my career at Burroughs Corporation (now Unisys). It was filled with hardware and software engineers from around the world. Despite the company's troubles (or perhaps because of them), it was a great training ground. It was a fact-based organization, and the engineering culture extended throughout the company.

The finance team was more buttoned-up than the average number crunchers because they reported to engineers, who would call them out if their numbers were wrong by even a little bit. In turn, the finance team wouldn't hesitate to call out an engineer. Part of my tenure with the company was in the marketing department—market research, to be precise. This team knew market history and trends—perhaps to a fault as they were so grounded in the past they seemed to struggle to look toward the future. (The company wasn't known for its foresight and forward thinking on the marketing side.) That said, the entire company culture focused on facts and on solving problems, which it did extraordinarily well.

Whenever you're dealing with a business problem, it's important to start with the facts. Whether the problem is in sales, marketing, finance, operations, or human resources, facts are critical to understanding the problem. It is impossible for a businessperson to make progress and develop a solution unless he or she has a firm grasp on the situation. And that is not possible when one is dealing only with anecdotal evidence.

Too regularly, people cite a few examples (which are pieces of the puzzle) and try to draw conclusions about the whole picture. The problem is that although they might get it right, it is more likely that they will not. Basing business decisions on a few stories or examples leads to conclusions based upon faulty assumptions.

Get the whole story. Make sure that you understand all the facts. Many readers may remember the story about the three blind men walking around the elephant, each feeling different parts of it and coming to different conclusions about what they were touching. It can often feel like this when you are trying to herd facts (often, about as difficult as herding cats) to gather sufficient data for analysis.

Gathering good facts is 80% to 90% of problem solving. Last week, the president of one of my client companies asked an excellent question during a meeting. The financial manager had spent four hours gathering the data and assembling it in a way that made it easy for us to analyze. Frankly, the analysis part took me about 20 minutes (plus more than 20 years of experience), but that was only because we had assembled all the data first.

▶ *Determine what facts you need to assess the situation. Gather and organize them. Solid analysis and the solution will flow from there.*

A Clerical Error Causes Bankruptcy

Recently I read an article about a company that sought protection under Chapter 11 bankruptcy laws for a clerical error. As they say, you just can't make this stuff up. The headline actually blamed the bankruptcy on tax bills that arose as a result of the clerical error. To suggest that either tax bills or clerical errors are the root cause of a company's failure is foolish. Tax bills (in this case for employment taxes) aren't a surprise. They are a cost of doing business. I assume this is a case of management and its lawyers trying to put some spin on the problem for the public. Of course, it could be the case that they actually believe this.

The root cause really is some combination of not being able to make the business model work in the current economic environment and management's being asleep at the wheel. Given the spurious comments from management and their counsel, I'm betting on the latter.

A relationship exists between net income and cash. The exact relationship depends on many factors. For example, growth businesses can be net income positive but need cash to support investments in inventory, capital expenditures, and expansion. For a business that is relatively stable, with little capital investment requirement, the relationship between net income and the change in cash might be one to one. In other words, depreciation might roughly offset new capital investment. Receivables and payables might vary on a month-to-month basis, but over the course of several months or a year they don't change very much. Alternatively, it might be a business in which most customers pay by cash or credit card, meaning that the business operates with virtually no accounts receivable. In any event, management should understand the relationship between net income and cash flow. To the extent that the business is not behaving accordingly, that is a huge red flag.

Furthermore, management should understand all the costs of running the business and know whether they are being recorded properly each month. Will there be accounting mistakes and clerical errors in a business? Yes. One of my client companies records approximately 30,000 transactions every month. At 99.9% accuracy, that would be 30 mistakes per month. At 99.99% accuracy, that would be three mistakes per month. Truthfully, we're operating somewhere in the middle of that band and working on automating more so that we run virtually mistake-free. That being said, none of the 10 or so errors among those 30,000 transactions are material. The very fact that we know about them says that we have a process that finds and fixes them (often before we close the books). Even if left unchecked, they wouldn't have a material effect on the financial statements. If it were material (and something that could put a company into bankruptcy is undoubtedly material), the error would be found and fixed.

It is the responsibility of management to properly present the financial condition of the company through monthly financial reporting. For management to suggest that they didn't understand the costs of running the business or the financial condition of the firm is simply an indication that they have abdicated their responsibilities. These people should be replaced without hesitation.

▶ *If you understand your business, you'll catch the clerical errors.*

Juggling Cash

There is no surer symptom of an unhealthy business than its being forced to juggle cash. Quite simply, this means that they are running so tight on cash every day that they are making conscious decisions as to who does and does not get paid based upon daily cash receipts. This process is incredibly time-consuming, prone to error, stressful for those working the process, and it adds absolutely no long-term value to the business. That said, I see businesses that have allowed themselves to get into this position on a regular basis. For perspective, a healthy business pays approved invoices within terms because it has the resources to do so. The process is simple and quick.

The problem often stems from a business that is undercapitalized because of a lack of equity capital put into the business, too much money being pulled out when times were good (leaving little reserve capacity), or a history of sustained losses that have eroded the equity capital base and pushed up borrowing. Frequently, the company is now at its debt limits and is forced to juggle cash to make payroll and keep key vendors happy. This is otherwise known as robbing Peter to pay Paul, or in more recent times, using Visa to pay MasterCard.

This process is expensive and takes a toll on the organization's psyche. I have seen very capable controllers spend almost all their time on this process while being forced to ignore cost-saving opportunities and efficiency initiatives that would help in the long term. They are moving cash among various accounts and entities, trying to collect from customers a few days sooner, and stringing out vendors as long as possible. Costs mount in terms of late fees, credit card charges, interest, penalties, and the like, but these pale in comparison to the real cost, which is staff time.

Vendors become less responsive, and when they are healthy enough they will significantly tighten terms and even fire the company, refusing to do business with people who are slow pay. Unhealthy vendors will continue to work with you, hoping that things will turn around, because they feel that they need to keep recording revenue even when payments are late. Usually, this weakens their financial position, too. At times, you can have a vendor help you through this period, but that requires transparency and honoring commitments when you make them. I've worked in businesses healthy enough to help a struggling customer, and it can be a win-win. I have also fired customers who were high touch, slow pay, and generally unprofitable. Frankly, it's a great feeling to take that step.

If you find yourself juggling cash, I would encourage you to step back and try to determine the root causes. Look at your recent profitability and capitalization. Both of those must be honest assessments.

Looking at profitability requires a solid balance sheet review. Is your inventory correctly valued? Are all your receivables collectable? Or, is there a proper reserve for collection issues? Are all your liabilities recorded? Does depreciation allow for capital replacement? Have you ignored maintenance issues for so long that there is a ticking time bomb out there waiting to go off?

Your banker will welcome a conversation on your capital structure and the appropriate amount of leverage for a company of your size, life cycle, and industry.

▶ *Stop juggling cash . . . solve the real problem.*

Questions

My work day is filled with questions. Whether I am the one asking the questions or answering them depends upon the day, the client, and the specific role I am playing. But in any case, the underlying motivation is almost always the same: how do we improve the business?

Perhaps every question sent through email, voicemail, text message, IM, fax, memo, and so forth ought to begin with the phrase, "To help me better understand and improve the business, would you please . . ." But the truth is that almost none of them begin this way.

As a result, it's easy for people to become offended by some of the questions that are being asked and the implied tone in the questions. This happens to all of us, and it can be more frustrating than the question itself. With that in mind, it's worthwhile to take a step back and remind ourselves of the actual motivation, which is to better understand or improve the business.

Most major business decisions are made by getting input from people with various backgrounds. The required expertise may include product, technical, finance, sales, marketing, manufacturing, operations, and other departments. Even in the same company, and even when that company is small, people from various disciplines can speak "different languages." Terms, phrases, and abbreviations that may be clear to people who work together all day may not be clear to people from other departments or to people who operate outside the company walls such as bankers, board members, consultants, and the like.

As a result, it's critical that people do their best to answer questions in a way that is clear to the person doing the asking. This means taking extra time to provide information and detail that may be second nature to the people answering. It may also mean referring back to the last conversation and reminding them of the context and a few of the basic facts that they may have forgotten.

For example, I recently got a request from a client to spend $5,000 on capital equipment for them. While this request was fairly well presented, I still went back and asked how it tied to the capital equipment budget we had reviewed the prior week before signing off on the request. I wanted to make sure it was for a budgeted item and that the amount was in line with our earlier discussion.

It's also important to keep in mind that the answers to questions tend to beget more questions. As people build their understanding of the business, they will continually drill down to the next level of detail. And if a question remains unanswered, it's a pretty good bet that it will keep coming up until it is answered.

So, the next time that you are answering a business question, perhaps the same question more than once, remember that it's probably worth a few extra minutes to provide the context needed so that the person asking clearly understands the answer. And even then, be ready for the follow-up.

▶ *If you try to understand what the underlying reason for the question, you can give a much better answer.*

Mark It On Your Calendar

Let me challenge you to do something differently right now. Book an appointment on your calendar for next Friday morning from 9:00 a.m. until 11:00 a.m. Send the appointment to your controller, bookkeeper, CPA, or whoever prepares your monthly financial statements. Tell them you want to spend two hours together reviewing last month's results.

Tell them to come prepared with the monthly income statement, balance sheet, and statement of cash flows. You also want to see month-to-month trends on the income statement and the balance sheet from the beginning of the year. Ask how last month's results differed from the month before it and why. Did you have a budget or plan? If so, how did last month compare?

Start at the top. Review revenue, and take the time to explore each line item if you have more than one. You don't just want to know the amount of the difference, but why it was different. What can be done to drive revenue?

Carefully consider each expense line item as well. Were expenses up or down for a reason? What can be done to improve the ratio of expenses to revenue? Which line items are fixed—that is, they do not vary with short-term volume changes—and which line items move relative to changes in revenue?

Look at the balance sheet. Are receivables being collected? Are vendors being paid in a timely manner? Were there any investments in capital equipment? Are you booking depreciation on a monthly basis? Are you covering the costs of wear and tear on your fixed assets so that there is enough money in the bank to pay for new machinery and equipment when your current equipment has to be replaced?

The cash flow statement explains the difference between profit and changes in cash. Admittedly, it can be difficult to read the first time. Muddle through it if you must. You'll understand it better next month.

Finally, what was the return on the capital you have invested in your business? Was it sufficient for the risk that you're incurring or would you have been better off putting your money into CDs? If you own and work in the business, have you been fairly paid for the time that you've invested?

▶ *By the way, if you're told this information isn't available, that's a big, red flag! Find out why, today!*

CHAPTER 10

Looking Outside Your Four Walls

The world isn't stagnant. And if management doesn't spend time thinking about how outside events and competitors affect the company's opportunities, then it will have ceded control to outside influences.

Are You Working On The Business?

Change

Watch For Red Flags

Working With Your Banker

What's Your Right To Exist?

Differentiate

Don't Just Survive. Thrive!

Are You Working On The Business?

A question that is not asked frequently enough, particularly of small business owners, is whether they are working *on* the business or working *in* the business. While the distinction may appear small, it is critically important.

Too many small business owners find themselves working *in* the business. This means they are working on day-to-day operational issues. They are interacting with customers, employees, and vendors. They are dealing with near-term financial issues. They may actually be responsible for a major functional area of the business rather than having someone take care of it for them and only getting involved in key decisions.

While resources are always tight in small businesses (and they are also tight in well run large businesses), if a business is to rise to the next level, a substantial amount of time must be spent thinking and acting on the issues that will help the business get there. This is what is generally meant as working *on* the business.

Working on the business is about opening up new sales and distribution channels as opposed to chasing the next sale. It is working with your team to develop a long-range strategic and financial plan. It is understanding the sustainable growth model of the business. It is having discussions with the board about forming strategic alliances that could help the company in the long term. It is thinking about where the market is going and being ready for, or leading, marketplace shifts. It is about knowing what customers need, how they perceive your product or service against those needs, and how you can deliver better against any gap. It is about understanding the overall competitive landscape. And it is about understanding the enterprise value that you are creating.

Unless the CEO and top management team spend time and energy working on long-term strategic business issues, they are likely to find themselves doing the same thing over and over, year after year, with about the same result. A good business doesn't stand still. It is always striving to move forward.

When resources are tight and time is limited (and both of these circumstances are usually the case) it is always difficult to find time for problems that don't affect the business today or tomorrow. But without the foresight to focus on the bigger picture, it is unlikely that the business will move forward in any meaningful way.

Ask yourself: what you are doing today which will alter the course of your business over the next three to five years? If the answer is nothing, then carve out the time to tackle some of the long-term issues that are important to the business. You'll be glad that you did.

▶ *Work on the business!*

Change

I often deal with change, and I see companies at both ends of the spectrum when it comes to attitudes about change. Some are in a constant state of flux, desperately trying to change in an effort to find something that works. Others are so afraid of change they won't try anything new. (I consulted for one company that in 2010 still was using green paper ledger sheets for their accounting.)

Some businesses try to do a little bit of everything and are not doing anything well, which is almost always a recipe for disaster. When companies don't commit to goals and objectives, it is easy for them to lose their way. They may start down a path only to change direction before they are able to see results. They are always sticking their toe in the water to gauge the temperature but never diving in and committing to an idea or objective. They are dabbling. They have tried to change so many times that future attempts are lost on the organization. These are companies that are in a constant state of flux. Chaos rules.

At the other end of the spectrum are companies afraid of committing to change. Usually guided by a single majority owner, they continue to do things the way they have always done them.

As a result, their market share erodes or they end up owning 100% of a shrinking market. Their competitors have walked away. In rare cases this may be a lucrative spot, but in most they are serving a handful of customers who also have refused to change. The company is serving the current owner but does not have a robust future, and it won't have much of a future unless the next generation of management shakes things up and moves the company forward.

Let's say that your company is wrapping up activity for the current year and thinking about the next. This is a natural time to ask yourself what you want the company to look like at the end of next year. Will you be satisfied if your company looks the same at the end of next year as it does today?

To be truly successful, you have to commit to an objective. If your company dabbles and is in a constant state of flux, it's vital to decide on a few key priorities and stick to them. On the other hand, if yours is one of those companies that is afraid to change, I'd encourage you to start making incremental changes to build momentum.

Meaningful change is hard. But anything worthwhile comes at a price.

▶ *What do you want to change?*

Watch For Red Flags

Some years ago, I was offered an opportunity to join a well-funded start-up company. As part of my due diligence, I read the business plan and shared it with a trusted advisor for help in evaluating the company. We talked about some specific concerns. And as we talked, it was clear that I was weighing my personal desires—to move to a new city, to get a much-needed change from big corporate environments to a smaller company—more heavily than the business plan. I won't forget his words to me during one of our calls. He said, "There are red flags. You can choose to ignore them by calling them pink or magenta, but we both know that they are red flags."

For example, when a company files for bankruptcy protection, this is not the first sign that they are financially troubled. While I empathize with anyone who is forced to recover through the bankruptcy process, it's probably fair to suggest that at least some of these suppliers chose to ignore the red flags that were in front of them. Or, as I had done, they chose to believe that the flags weren't actually red, but rather pink, magenta, or some other color that suggested a less dire situation.

I am willing to bet that many of the creditors extended the bankrupt company many months of credit. I think an interesting question is how many of these vendors consciously evaluated the risks of extending further credit in light of slow payment for past goods or services and how many simply chose to ignore the warning signs that were in front of them? It's likely that in most cases, vendors chose to believe the best case scenario of increased business and profits to follow (well, at least as soon as they got paid). Knowingly or unknowingly, those extending significant credit were acting as miniature venture capital firms and deserved to earn returns appropriate for the risks they were incurring.

When customers aren't making timely payments, they are effectively asking you, the vendor, to act as a lender. In the case of the bankrupt company, suppliers weren't just supplying short-term, low-risk financing; they were effectively supplying high-risk venture funding. If they didn't realize the risks that they were taking, they certainly couldn't ask for an appropriate return for that risk.

It is critical to recognize that choosing to accept the risks of extending significant financing to customers is a business decision that deserves careful consideration. Every situation is different, and no one answer can address every situation. Extending credit to a growing customer could secure a long-term relationship and prove very profitable. However, simply choosing to ignore the red flags is clearly a bad decision. Even if things turn out well in the end, it will be due to luck rather than to good business judgment.

In my case, I ignored the red flags. I quelled my inner voice and told myself that other people who read the business plan were smarter or understood it better. Every time that I have done this, I've regretted it, even when things turn out well in the end.

▶ *Never ignore red flags. Heed their warnings. Understand, evaluate, and make a thoughtful decision.*

Working With Your Banker

Believe it or not, your banker wants to lend you money and wants to see your business grow. That's how they earn their money. They borrow from depositors and pay them a rate of interest, and then they lend to businesses at a higher rate. At a deeper level, banking is obviously much more complicated, but at some level it is very simple (like most businesses).

That said, for the bank to make a reasonable return, they have to manage their risk, meaning that they must adhere to their underwriting guidelines and make reasonable judgments before lending. This is why banks have committees to approve loans.

Repeatedly, I find clients telling me that their bank won't work with them. This usually means that they won't increase their credit lines. This is usually followed by the comment that the banker "just doesn't understand our business." Well, that may or may not be true. The banker probably doesn't understand your business as well as you. Nor should you expect him to. After all, he first and foremost understands banking. On the other hand, I have at times seen bankers demonstrate a better understanding of a business than the owner.

Generally, however, it is the job of management to help the banker understand the business. Typically, when I hear a complaint about the banker, I ask to see the write-up that is sent with the financial statements. Often, I get a blank stare (or silence if we are on a phone call). In addition, it is not uncommon for financial statements to be poorly presented (too much or too little detail, no logical order, poorly formatted, and so forth) or simply incomplete, (commonly missing the statement of cash flows or comparisons to a year ago or budget). How can the banker represent the company at their lending committee meeting if management is not giving them the tools to do so?

When you are presenting financial information to your banker, it should be timely and well prepared, and it should include all financial statements (income statement, balance sheet and statement of cash flows), as well as comparisons to the prior period (last month, last quarter, or a year ago), and/or budget, as appropriate. It also needs to come with a management discussion and analysis, which explains how the business is performing. This allows the banker to understand your business and represent you within the bank. It also allows them to do their job better because they can ask better questions about your business, inasmuch as most of the basics will be covered in the memo.

Banks have underwriting guidelines that change from time to time because of market conditions and issues internal to the bank. But guidelines are just that; they are not necessarily cast in stone. By providing an explanation of the financial statements, management demonstrates that they understand the financial position of the business as well as the bank's perspective. The better that management can do this job, the more likely it is that the bank will make an exception to its guidelines if and when that is necessary.

Banks lend to people. Therefore, the relationship between management and the bank is key. The better that relationship, the better the bank can help the business. Ultimately, that is what you want from your banker and what bankers want to provide to you as their client.

▶ *Help your banker help you.*

What's Your Right To Exist?

I believe that every business must earn its right to exist in the marketplace. Yes, I said earn. No business has an inalienable right to exist. Rather, in a competitive marketplace, that right has to be earned day in and day out.

Every business must ask itself how it earns this right. More important, it should also ask its customers. What specific niche does the business serve in the marketplace? What does it do better than any of its competitors? Does it compete solely on price (a valid strategy)? Ultimately, why do customers choose to spend their dollars with the company?

Another way of asking this question is: what is the core competency of the business? What does it do better than anyone else?

Sometimes, a business is surrounded by competitors but delivers excellent service. They are among the best of the best. There may be room for many or just a few in the particular market, but delivering outstanding service at a fair price—and that is not necessarily a low price—is a proven strategy. Sometimes a business delivers such good service that they are able to dominate the marketplace.

Other times, price leadership may be the strategy. There is usually room for competitors that offer a good product or service—not the very best, but good—but at a great price. Customers who are price sensitive or to whom good enough is satisfactory will frequent this business.

Another unique position in the marketplace might stem from geography. I frequent a drive-through car wash, and although they offer excellent service, it's more important to me that they occupy a unique geographic advantage. Customers would be willing to travel only a certain distance to a competitor regardless of the advantages in price or service that they might offer.

When answering questions about market positions, right to exist, and why competitors frequent a business, think broadly about the marketplace. Thinking broadly opens up a world of possibilities. Think about the differences between shopping at Nordstrom and at Walmart, for example. The differences are striking, but both have a place in the market. Of course, you can make an argument that these two retailers are not competitors, because clearly they are targeting very different segments of the marketplace. But at some level, they do compete—after all, you can buy a pair of socks at both.

When a business asks itself tough, probing questions about its position in the marketplace, it can use the answers in the strategic planning process to help determine how it can and should profitably grow. Ultimately, this is the most important question a business must answer, and it is the primary responsibility of leadership.

▶ *How does your business earn its right to exist in the marketplace?*

Differentiate

How do you differentiate your product or service? Even better, how do your customers perceive the differentiation between you and your competitors? These are important questions. And you should answer the first before you attempt to answer the second. Doing so will give you a basis for determining whether you perceive your business in the same way as your customers perceive it. Don't be surprised if your customers perceive your product or service differently than you.

And in case anyone reading this has forgotten: the customer is always right. I can think of a number of businesses that were arrogant enough to believe that the customer "didn't get it." Frankly, they may have been right. But it doesn't matter. The customers took their dollars elsewhere and those arrogant businesses exist no more.

Find out why customers use your product or service and how you can improve upon it. What keeps them coming back, and what will bring them back more frequently? What will incite them to recommend your business to someone else?

Differentiation is essential in both good times and bad. In good times, it allows companies to enjoy higher volumes, profit margins, and expansion. In bad times, it can be the difference between life and death. Generally, players that are able to differentiate themselves from their competitors survive. Customers find a reason to go there in good times and bad. Companies that deliver a me-too experience (one that is about the same as that which you can get from any of their competitors with no differentiating characteristics) don't build customer loyalty. In good times, customers might try someplace else in the hopes of having a better experience. In bad times, customers are all the more tempted to price shop or forgo their purchase altogether.

Think of some recent closures and ask yourself if they differentiated in the marketplace. Linens-N-Things closed while Bed Bath & Beyond survived. Given the lack of differentiation between the stores, it's not surprising that one of them was left behind. From a consumer perspective, I can't think of a reason to favor one over the other.

I think the story is similar with Circuit City which closed while Best Buy survived. Two big-box retailers were fighting in a crowded space. From my home, I could get to either one easily, but I can't think of a single compelling reason to have chosen one over the other.

Does anyone remember Hechinger's or Builder's Square? They were two of the early big-box home improvement centers that were beaten by competitors (Lowe's and Home Depot) who, as far as I can tell, simply built bigger boxes.

A few companies with closed stores continue to exist as online retailers, but they are mere shadows of their former selves. In any space, businesses need to earn consumers' dollars and therefore the right to exist. Without a strong differentiation from competitors, a business is much more vulnerable and therefore more likely to suffer from pricing pressures, loss of market share, and eventual failure.

▶ *How does your business differentiate itself from the competition?*

Don't Just Survive . . . Thrive

In financially tumultuous years (2008–2009, for example), it's easy to imagine that many companies think about what it will take to survive the year. While it's obviously critical that you survive, you also need to think about setting your sights a little higher. Ask yourself: what will it take to thrive next year and beyond?

While that might seem like a difficult if not impossible notion to contemplate, especially in some industries, difficult times often make for opportunities. During slow economic times, there is normally a shake-out of the weakest players in every industry. While that can be unfortunate, it's also part of the economic reality in which we live. But when the business cycle turns, as it invariably will, there will be more opportunities for those that remain. The question at hand is: what can you do today to position yourself for a stronger tomorrow?

- Is this the time to think about picking up new talent that may now be available?

- Can you use any slowdown in your core business to develop new lines of products or services by deploying people and resources to other areas?
- If your staff has less work to do than usual, can that time be used for training or to upgrade their skills?
- Are there opportunities to do more for your current customers?
- Might there be some areas where you should increase spending as opposed to thinking only of cutting back?
- Is there an opportunity to purchase a struggling competitor?

I realize that this is somewhat out-of-the-box thinking, but that is what is required for a company to be successful. The future will likely present a number of challenges for both big and small companies. How companies respond to those challenges will be the difference between those that survive and those that are poised to thrive when the economy improves.

Search for the negatives in your business and eliminate them. Whether it is relationships with underperforming vendors, employees, or even problem customers, now is not the time to be carrying extra baggage. Take corrective action. There are others who would welcome a relationship with your business during difficult times.

Set your sights high. Look for the opportunities that difficult times present and take advantage of them to the greatest extent possible. Search for ways to become a stronger player in your marketplace. Make yourself memorable to your customers and give them a reason to maintain an ongoing relationship with you.

▶ *What can you do to thrive versus simply survive?*

CHAPTER 11

Strategy And The Will To Succeed

Of all the challenges in business, keeping people motivated (including yourself) is among the most difficult. Taking time to think about strategic issues is a chance to renew the spirit and the will to succeed as well as to reinvigorate the organization.

• Let's Talk Strategy

• It's About Will

• Stay Motivated

Let's Talk Strategy

Whatever the forum, you owe it to your business to get away from the day-to-day issues of running your company and focus on the big picture. Recall from the previous chapter the question of whether you are working on your business or in your business? The distinction is important. Too often, business leaders find themselves so enmeshed in daily operations that they are not doing what they are really supposed to be doing, which is guiding the business.

Spending a day, or even better a week or more, focusing solely on the strategy of your business can be a rewarding experience. This can be done either exclusively with members of your management team or during a sponsored forum or similar local event. The advantage of attending an event is that there is an outside influence as well as course material that poses questions about different types of businesses and gives you a chance to ask yourself similar questions about your own business.

More important, there is likely to be a framework from which to have strategic discussions with your entire team at a later date. At a Washington University in St. Louis program on strategic planning that I attended, the speaker suggested a framework that consisted of four strategic/cultural platforms:

- ***Collaborative:*** integration, empowerment and teamwork.

- ***Creative:*** change oriented and externally focused.

- ***Control:*** standards and metrics based. Focus on efficiency.

- ***Competitive:*** speed, financial returns, and customer need.

While no organization exclusively expresses only one characteristic—all have some degrees from each of the four areas—most organizations have a dominant trait. While I can't do justice to a full-day seminar in such a short space, I want to present these ideas as food for thought.

Regardless of the way in which you choose to frame your strategic discussions, I would encourage every leadership team to invest the time to engage in strategic discussions that provide the opportunity to think differently about the business.

Does your finance leader help you to think strategically? Rather than just providing a page full of numbers, can they offer insightful thoughts about what the numbers mean? More important, can they take it to the next level and suggest actions that the company should take to improve its position in the marketplace?

▶ *Your business needs and deserves strategic thinking!*

It's About Will

When it comes to solving problems, it's all about will.

Any business can be fixed. Now, that's a bold statement, and it might be hard to believe. And while there are no doubt exceptions, I believe that as a general rule most businesses can be fixed or at least substantially improved.

In almost every situation in which I've seen a business languishing, it's because the powers that be simply don't have the will to fix the problems. There are three issues that must be faced in addressing any problem:

1. ***Define:*** truly know and understand the problem based upon facts.

2. ***Solve:*** develop one or more cost-effective solutions.

3. ***Implement:*** take action or fix the problem.

In most organizations, almost everyone thinks they know the problems as well as the potential solutions. Frequently, however, they lack the hard evidence needed to gain agreement on defining the problem, whether that agreement is in the form of organization consensus or executive buy-in. The problem never gets resolved because there are so many different opinions as to what the problem is. This is one of the reasons I am such a big advocate of having fact-based discussions.

The next level of difficulty, of course, is the solution. Generally, people spend so much time griping about the problem that they spend almost no time on the possible solutions. There is a huge difference between analyzing a problem along with the potential solutions and simply complaining about it. Anecdotal evidence is no substitute for analysis. Usually, if you can gain agreement on the definition of the problem, you will have made substantial progress toward developing potential solutions.

Taking action is truly the hard part. It requires the will of the key players to make the hard decisions. When an organization fails to take action, it is often because the minor, day-to-day, annoying pain of any problem seems to pale in comparison to the perceived gut-wrenching pain of a major organizational change. It's like that noise in your car that you hear every day. You know something is wrong, but it doesn't appear to be causing any major problems. Then, one day, the transmission falls out, and now there really is a major problem. The same holds true in companies. What appear to be small problems chip away at the health of the organization on a daily basis. Over time, the impact is enormous.

If your business is languishing, or it's flourishing but you're not sure it's living up to its true potential, think about solving some of those "small" problems in your organization.

▶ *Do you have the will to solve problems?*

Stay Motivated

Motivating yourself and others in your company is one of the most impactful things that a leader can do. Unfortunately, staying motivated can be difficult, and losing motivation is all too easy. Day-to-day problems can sap your motivation and distract you from long-term problems of greater importance.

Maybe you have attended an all-day motivational seminar with nationally known speakers. The problem with these one-day events is how they play out in the days and weeks afterward. Getting motivated is one thing; staying motivated is quite another.

It is a rare few who don't struggle with motivation from time to time. It is essential to have sources of motivation that you can tap. I have twice had the opportunity to visit the United States Military Academy at West Point to run as a civilian behind the teams participating in the Sandhurst Military Skills competition. Both were exceptional experiences. There are few places on earth as motivated as our nation's military academies. In the summer I have the opportunity to work out three mornings a week in the company of nearly two dozen highly motivated men and women who are training with the St. Louis Military Officer Support Foundation.

Each of these young men and women is currently enrolled in one of the academies, will be entering in the fall, or is a recent graduate already serving our country and home on leave. It is an exceptional group and it's hard not to give your best when you are surrounded by others who are doing so.

Whatever your source of motivation may be, it's critical to find a way to maintain your motivational levels and replenish them as needed.

As you head back to the office, ask yourself whether you are working with a motivated group of people. Are you leading by example and providing the motivational spark needed for yourself and those around you? What sources of motivation can you find that will have a lasting effect?

▶ *How do you stay motivated?*

CHAPTER 12

Are Your Struggles Internal?

Too many times, the biggest enemy a company faces is internal. Employees aren't armed with the facts. They are competing against each other and just don't understand the problems that other departments face or how to help each other compete against the real enemy—the competition.

- Is Ignorance Bliss?

- The CFO Who Knew Too Much

- Competing Silos

- Get The Answers You Want

- Critical Skills In The C-Suite

- Effective Boards

Is Ignorance Bliss?

There is a saying that ignorance is bliss. But is it really? I routinely see key managers in organizations operating with little or no knowledge of the company's financial situation. While this may allow them to go about their duties without the burden of understanding the financial position of the company, it doesn't allow them to help the business as much as they should.

While I'm not suggesting that everyone in the organization should have a detailed understanding of financial performance, it is important for key managers to have a working knowledge of the financial facts so that they can make informed business decisions. Too often, particularly in poorly performing organizations, I see companies in which the CEO tries to shelter the rest of the organization from dealing with the facts.

On the flip side, successful organizations tend to share financial performance measures much more broadly than do poorly performing organizations. I don't think this is coincidence. Nor do I think it is because successful organizations are proud to share their results while poor performing are ashamed to do so, even though that is probably true. I think there is a cause-and-effect relationship.

Organizations that find a way to share financial performance measures and, more important, reward employees for overall performance, get better results. Employees throughout the organization can work toward a common goal and have a financial perspective, if not a detailed understanding, for decision making. They comprehend better why management takes certain actions and can make decisions that are consistent with those of senior management.

If the people representing the grass roots of the organization have no appreciation for the financial performance of the firm, you often find them making decisions that are in direct opposition to those that senior management is making. Nowhere is this more apparent than in struggling organizations in which employees are empowered to make decisions about spending but lack the proper context with which to make those decisions.

Imagine trying to row a boat with other people if there were no agreement on which direction you wanted the boat to go. How effective do you think you would be, compared to a boat with people all rowing in the same direction at the same pace?

▶ *Think about your organization. Is ignorance really bliss?*

The CFO Who Knew Too Much

Some time ago, I was in a meeting as the new acting/interim/ fractional CFO for a company. Truthfully, I am not sure how best to describe the role. Major investors had asked me to step in and basically informed management that I was coming aboard. Management was less than pleased. Obviously, there was a reason for my injection into the company, and it wasn't to count all the money they were making. Things had been going badly for some time, and there wasn't much optimism about the future. It's not the first time I've accepted such an assignment, and I'm sure it won't be the last.

Shortly after coming on board, I was in a meeting with the CEO and major investors. Much of the meeting focused on operational issues that were causing the cash burn. While I hadn't been to the plant yet (something I always try to do immediately), I was still pretty well versed on the problems they were facing. At one point during the meeting, I offered a suggestion to improve operations. I had another client dealing with a similar issue and had been at their plant days earlier. As always, part of my visit with that team included walking the plant and discussing operational issues with others on the management team as well as the rank and file.

When I offered my suggestion, the CEO responded with, "That's an obvious solution." He was right . . . what I suggested wasn't rocket science. Yet, he had failed to take action on something that was obvious because he didn't grasp the economic impact of solving the problem.

His feedback after the meeting was that I "knew too much about operations." Sometimes all you can do is shake your head. I got the company through a major milestone and then departed. To this day, they struggle, and they will continue to struggle until they change management.

The CFO can't know too much. The primary role of the CFO is to understand the business and the economics of the decisions being made. These decisions need to be team based, with input from all the major disciplines in the firm. For the CFO to have valid input, they need to fully comprehend the implications of decisions just as much as the marketing or operational person needs to have an understanding of finance. Executives need to be well-rounded, and that is particularly indispensable in the role of CFO.

Being CFO is not about debits and credits. The role of the CFO is about adding strategic value to the firm and playing a major role in the decision-making process. Money is a finite resource, and how that resource is deployed determines the outcome of the firm.

▶ *You need a CFO who can help you make decisions that add long-term strategic value to the firm. Why settle for anything less?*

Competing Silos

One of the side effects of lacking perspective on your company's financial situation is silos within the organization. While the lack of financial perspective isn't the sole cause of a "siloed" organization, I certainly believe it is a contributing factor.

The silo effect is people working with only their own or their department's goals in mind, in many instances to the detriment of other departments or even the entire organization. I almost always find that there is a lack of perspective on financial performance for the organization as a whole. People simply don't grasp the bigger picture. It's often not their fault; no one has ever given them the data and facts, even in a limited fashion.

Rather than pulling together and fighting against the competition, people end up fighting with each other for internal resources. Victories are about winning vis-à-vis other departments. People consider it a win when they get to add a person and another department doesn't, when they get above-average raises for their people, or when one department gets new computers while another doesn't. These so-called "victories" are often based upon the political influence of department heads (i.e., how effectively they lobby their positions) as opposed to the optimum allocation of resources within an organization. This is destructive to the organization, causes further competition and resentment by the "losing" departments, and contributes to an apathetic attitude toward the decision-making process.

I believe that people are naturally competitive. So why not give them a common enemy to compete against? Better that than to have them competing with each other (to the detriment of the business).

There is a story that at one point in the history of Anheuser-Busch Companies, they launched a "Kill Miller" campaign. Think about that. Two words and everyone in the company knew the objective. Moreover, it could be measured in terms of market share. In the long run, everyone would know how the company was doing in its quest.

I spent five years at LensCrafters. The leadership team there clearly knew how to focus the organization's competitive juices toward company objectives. There were times when it was simply inspiring to see the entire organization focus on an objective and exhilarating to be part of accomplishing the goal.

If it is a given that people in your organization are going to compete—and I believe that to be the case—then give them something to compete against that will benefit the business. Make sure they know that the true competition is about winning customers in the marketplace and providing better products and services than the next guy. It's not about who gets a new desk or office chair or which department gets a slightly bigger share of the raise pool.

▶ *If you don't find an external competitor . . . internal competition is sure to develop.*

Get The Answer You Want

During any given week, I get multiple requests like, "Can we spend $2,500 on ABC?" or, "We need to buy XYZ and it's going to cost $12,000."

My response is almost always the same: what are our options? Is this the best solution, given where we are today? Have we gotten other prices? What happens if we don't spend the money? What's our return if we do spend the money? Does it to help bring in extra revenue? Does the expenditure save other costs? Does it meaningfully improve customer service? Why are you recommending that we spend this money?

Frequently, the person asking the question hasn't given a moment's thought to any of these questions. The most typical (and usually incredulous) reply is, "We've been doing it this way for years." For the record, "We've been doing it this way for years" is *never* an acceptable response to *any* CFO.

Afterward, the person who made the request can usually be heard saying something like, "Finance didn't approve the request." I guess that is factually accurate, but requests like these don't merit approval. So when the employee who submitted the request says that they are "waiting for Finance approval," the truth is that Finance is waiting for the employee to perform reasonable due diligence and present a thoughtful, sensible business case for the expenditure.

Do you want a fast response to your request? Try walking into any CFO's office with a request like this, preferably in writing: "I'm requesting an expenditure of $5,000 for Product X. I believe this is necessary because it will reduce the number of calls coming into customer service by 10%. While we can't eliminate any hard costs, it will give us more time to tackle other projects—specifically, improved reporting on trouble tickets. I've looked at other options, and there are competing products that start at $4,000. While the product I'm recommending isn't the cheapest, it is the industry leader, and our research indicates that it is superior to any of its competitors. I think the company is better served by spending a bit more than going with the lowest-cost solution."

Let me assure you, this kind of request (depending on the actual dollar amount, the budget, and so forth) will get attention and be quickly approved. It tells Finance that the person asking for the funds has thought about the request and performed reasonable due diligence. They are making a recommendation, not asking for permission. That's a very important distinction. It's so important, that I'm going to repeat it: *don't ask for permission; make a recommendation.*

When you seek funding, everyone knows that you want the answer to be yes, so why not make it easy for the supervisor to approve it? And if you are the person responsible for spending, due diligence is part of your job.

▶ *Give them the information they need and you'll get the answer you want.*

Critical Skills In The C-Suite

I believe that every C-Suite* executive needs three things, and that these hold true whether one is operating in a very small or very large company. While the bar is much higher at the top of Fortune 500 organizations than in smaller companies, the same skill sets are required to ensure that the organization is successful. Few things in business are as consequential as a well-functioning executive suite (although in small companies, the suite probably doesn't consist of the spacious offices, expensive furnishings, and executive assistants that make up a larger company C-suite).

First, all individuals on the executive team need bring to the table a domain expertise (finance, marketing, operations, human resources, and so forth). One of the reasons for their presence is that they are experts in their field. Furthermore, a broad cross section of all disciplines must be represented in the C-Suite. What business can be successful if it understands production but doesn't have a clue about how to market its product or service?

---

* C-Suite: A term that refers to a corporation's most important executives. So named because the titles of top executives usually start with the letter *C*, for chief, as in CFO.

Second, each and every executive must be well-rounded. They must have a working knowledge of other essential domain areas. The marketing executive must understand the finances of the business just as the finance executive needs to understand the marketing approach. If members of the executive team don't recognize and appreciate each other's worlds, then it is next to impossible for them to make the trade-offs that are inevitable in any business. Resources are finite, so there is always a balancing act as dollars are traded between different priorities. Unless all the executives have an appreciation for the other functions, then you have a land grab for resources, as opposed to decisions being made with the goal of advancing the company. I've seen this in companies both large and small.

Finally, every executive needs to demonstrate the Seven Critical Business Skills of the C-Suite. And every executive must have every skill set. Without even one of them, they simply cannot operate an optimum level.

1. **Vision.** Each executive must have a view of where they want the company and their particular department to be in the future. They must have a view of the environment in which they operate and be able to conceptualize how that might change in the future. Without vision, they are simply responding to the moment and, in all likelihood, remaining stagnant (or falling behind).

2. **Drive.** They must have the motivation to get to a new and better place. C-Suite executives are never satisfied with the status quo. They are seeking to improve performance in some way every day.

3. ***Problem Solving.*** They can grasp the problem that they are facing and develop a solution. And the solution must have a reasonable chance of success.

4. ***Prioritization.*** Executives have to ensure that the organization is focusing on things that matter. Numerous items take up our time, but being able to prioritize, not only for oneself but for the organization, is critical. The organization needs to work on items that will have a positive impact on the bottom line.

5. ***Delegation.*** Whether in a large or small business, no one person can do it all. It is necessary to be able to delegate and then step away and let someone else do the work. Recognize that they might not do it exactly as you would have done it. In the end, it is the result that counts, and your job is to help them get across the finish line.

6. ***Decision Making.*** Every day is filled with decisions: some big, some little. For a company to thrive, executives need to be able to process information and make decisions that are both timely and well thought out. I have seen executives who were considered decisive for the speed with which they made decisions, but their decisions lacked quality. On the other hand, I have seen executives who labored over a decision for so long that it was excruciating. Good decision making considers the information at hand and the time it takes to gather additional facts, and it is timely.

7. ***Communication.*** The ability to communicate effectively both inside and outside the organization is critical. Executives must be able to communicate their vision and their rationale for

decisions, and they must be able to motivate and lead those around them. They have to sell their ideas both internally and externally.

As you think about your executive team, consider whether each person has the necessary Seven Critical Business Skills. Are members of the C-Suite well-rounded? And is all the necessary domain expertise present in the C-Suite? If anything is lacking, the company is not living up to its full potential. Identify any gaps and fill them. Your future depends on it.

▶ *How does your C-Suite measure up?*

Effective Boards

The difference in company performance between one with an effective board of directors and one that is not effective can be dramatic. In the short run, it may seem like it is easier to have a lax board, but in the long run it will be far more difficult when the company has to face the music because of its poor performance.

Boards that are demanding can have a dramatic impact on the performance of the company. That said, board members need to do more than just ask questions or make superficial comments. (One of my favorite comments was that management should try to leverage current customers by doing more business with them— as though management hadn't thought of trying to have a deeper relationship with current customers.) But board members who can offer more than superficial comments and who ask intelligent, probing questions can add value, particularly when they have a deep knowledge of the industry or marketplace.

I recently had the experience of working with two companies at the same time that had very different boards. Management of the company with the stronger board took action—reluctantly at first, but they quickly embraced the direction the board wanted to go.

The change in profitability, within months, has been dramatic. The company is in a far better position because of the board. There are times when, despite the best efforts of the management team, they need the insights of those who can step back and see from a broader perspective. They can sometimes leverage knowledge of different companies and different board interactions.

At the same time, I am working with another company with a lax board that seems to take a wait-and-see approach. Although company results are not getting worse, they are not getting better. Underperformance (just like superior performance) is cumulative. The longer a company underperforms, the weaker its position, both financially and otherwise.

If you don't have a board, or if you find that your board is ineffective, it is up to management to do something about it. Add board members who are effective and who add value. Ask those who aren't effective to change their ways or else remove them from the board. Just as the board can demand change from management, so too can management demand change from its board members.

▶ *Insist upon an effective board.*

CHAPTER 13

There Is An "I" In Team

There may be no "I" in team, but every team is made up of a collection of individuals, and unless some individual leads that team to greatness, it is likely to fail. Moreover, if the team doesn't serve the needs of the individuals, then how can those same individuals meet the greater good of the team?

• The Differentiator

• The Weakest Link

• Watch The Strong Links Too

• Fun Versus Hard Work

• End The Debate: Decide

The Differentiator

Because of my fractional role, I have the opportunity to work with more management teams than most. I have consistently found that the one differentiator in the performance of a company is the quality and cohesiveness of the management team. The use of the word *team* is not by chance. While I could have used the term *members of management*, just having a number of senior managers around won't get the job done. Management is a team sport made up of various disciplines (operations, sales, marketing, finance, research, development, human resources, and so forth). Without a well-assembled team, the operation won't run smoothly. The performance and therefore the profitability of the organization won't be maximized.

I have seen cohesive, committed management teams that are underfunded, understaffed, and challenged with daunting problems not of their own making get the job done despite the odds being stacked against them. On the flip side, I have seen *members of management* with the wind at their back stumble and fail because of the lack of communication, coordination, and commitment.

Groups like this can make trivial tasks difficult. The bottom line is that I'll bet on the good management team any day of the week. I view this as the single most important contributing factor to the success to any company.

When looking at a business problem, whether you are on the outside looking in or are in the middle of the situation, take a moment to step back and observe how the management team is behaving.

Are they communicating with each other? Does everyone know in real time what is going on? Is there communication among the team and with outsiders, as appropriate? It is amazing how much good a little communication can do to avoid making bad problems worse. In business, people hate surprises. Why? Because a surprise is almost never good. It is much more likely to be bad news. Good news gets leaked early, and the reality is usually not quite as good as the early indicators suggest. Bad news tends to come from out of the blue, owing to a lack of communication. Rarely should it have truly been a surprise.

Is the management team coordinating? Do they have a well-thought-out plan? Is everyone making sure that all the bases are covered? In an age when we rely on email, texting, and cell phone communication, there is still no substitute for people sitting around the table, looking each other in the eye, and being absolutely certain that there is a common understanding of the problem, a complete discussion of potential solutions, and a coordinated plan of attack that will bring about a solution.

Most important, is the team committed? I am writing this at 6:30 a.m. on a Saturday morning. One of my companies is a day behind in achieving an operational milestone. I am absolutely certain that the management team is having their morning coffee, thinking about solutions to the problem, and heading to the plant if they are not already there. Their weekend will begin when the problem is solved. These guys are a cohesive team and truly committed.

▶ *Do you have a "management team" or just "members of management"?*

The Weakest Link

The weakest link is a potential problem that companies usually put into the risk category but which I think goes to the subject of business performance. Often, employers refer to the risks to the business if a certain individual were to leave the company. They'll openly wonder about what would happen if a certain employee "got hit by a bus." Well, in all of my years in the work force, I've been fortunate to never actually know of an employee who got hit by the proverbial bus. Of course, we all know that the real risk people are concerned about is what would happen if this person just up and quit one day with little notice. Again, this is something that rarely happens. Most employees are professional enough to give at least two weeks' notice. There may be times when they do not want to do so, but they recognize that it is in their long-term, best interest.

The underlying concern, of course, is that this individual is the only one who knows how to perform certain critical business functions, and therefore the organization is held hostage to him or her. These functions are usually not well-documented or understood by others. Unlike having employees get run over by buses, this is a phenomenon that I've seen time and again in the business world. And time and again, companies adapt. Usually, there is not so much that is a mystery (and others understand more than the weakest link led people to believe), and the customary two weeks notice is sufficient for companies to find a way to fill any gaps. Moreover, it's often the case that some of those critical, mysterious functions can be performed differently to reach the same result. Sometimes, they don't need to be performed at all.

I believe that the real concern with critical functions being understood by only one person is less about that person leaving the organization and more about day-to-day business performance. Often, this one person is a bottleneck to the rest of the organization. Their lack of action on a particular item can cause the entire company to grind to a halt. Other employees can become unproductive as they enter a state of waiting. More important, customers are kept waiting, resulting in lost revenue in the short term and lost customers in the long term, because they find another company that will provide more timely service. To add insult to injury, it is sometimes the case that the employee who is so critical in one area is an underperformer in others. Overall, the business would benefit if it were no longer held hostage by him or her.

In almost every company I've worked with, I've seen one employee who is that bottleneck. If you look around your organization, chances are that you'll find a bottleneck in a critical area who limits the performance of the entire organization.

One key to improving company performance is to search for and eliminate underperforming resources. It is an old saying but true that a chain is only as strong as its weakest link. The same holds true in any organization.

▶ *Do you have a weak link?*

Watch The Strong Links Too

Within a few hours of publishing my newsletter on the weakest link, I got an email from one of my readers. It stated: "This nails it for me. I get frustrated because I get overloaded and I know others are waiting on me. I used to be able to keep up, but it's just too much . . ." At first, I laughed. But then it dawned on me that not only can your weakest links be a bottleneck, but so can some of your strongest links.

The person who wrote to me is clearly a strong link. But the problem with strong links is that, over time, too much pressure can be put on their section of the chain. We all know that, unlike a real chain in which every link must support the same load, certain parts of an organization carry a bigger burden than others. So, while the answer for weak links is generally to get them out of the organization, the answer for strong links is quite different. Usually, the solution is to find a way to restructure their job so that they can add as much value as possible. In other words, they should be performing tasks that they are uniquely qualified to do, not something that could be delegated to others. This of course assumes that the strong links are willing to delegate. Sometimes they are not, and that can be the reason they are overloaded in the first place. Still, a solution must be found that keeps them from being bottlenecks.

More important, these people also need sufficient free time to be able to think about ways to improve their own function as well as the rest of the organization. Generally they can offer helpful input to areas outside of their own. When a strong link is so busy that all they can do is to keep up with the day-to-day demands placed upon them, then they don't have the free time to contribute in a more meaningful way. The lack of "thought time," a deficiency which has become increasingly pervasive in the business world, limits their contribution to the organization as well as their ability to grow their own career. This serves neither them nor the company well.

So while weak links can clearly limit an organization's performance, so can over-reliance on strong links. If you see someone in your organization who is generally a strong performer but is starting to become a bottleneck, then it is well worth your time to investigate further and understand both the root cause of this problem and what can be done to resolve the situation.

▶ *Even strong links can break.*

Fun Versus Hard Work

A s I have done many mornings, I was recently training with a group of military cadets and someone mentioned the word "fun." More specifically, they had said that the morning workout wasn't much fun. For the record, few among us consider our morning workout fun. If you push yourself, it's hard work. But the fun part is in the results.

The same goes with most business problems. Sure, there are days when business is fun, but most of the time it is just plain hard work. The fun part comes in seeing the results. Years ago I was working on an acquisition and the bookkeeper at the target company asked if I ever smiled at work and what made me happy. She had the accounting package open on her desktop, and I pointed to all the negative numbers in red ink. I told her that I'm happy when red ink turns black. That's when you know you have made an impact. It's hard to smile when you're awash in red ink.

I see businesses all the time that try to avoid the hard work part of running a business. They avoid the difficult decisions that incrementally improve a business. And make no mistake, most business improvement is incremental. It comes from doing countless small things better each day with an eye toward long-term improvement. In almost all cases, people are looking for a silver bullet: that one easy thing that will change their business from money-losing to profitable overnight. That silver bullet almost never exists.

Left unattended, small problems get worse.

- Management avoids dealing with the lazy employee because it is easier to let it slide. That employee's attitude infects another, and now the company has two bad employees.

- They avoid dealing with a slow-paying customer, hoping that the situation will resolve itself. Then payments stop altogether, and the account is a total write-off.

- They don't invest in better technology, hoping to get by with what they have. Then there is a system crash and the company is down for a day, or two, or more.

- They settle for inadequate financial reporting, since it has gotten them this far. Then the bank gets tired of it all and refuses to renew their line of credit.

Problems don't go away if left unattended. They get worse.

On the flip side, fixing one problem actually has the opposite effect. Getting rid of the lazy employee motivates others. Clamping down on a slow-paying customer forces them to pay you (although then they probably start slow-paying someone else). Upgrading technology allows people to complete work sooner with less frustration. Better financial reporting allows for a higher level of dialogue with the bank and true insight into business performance.

As problems are resolved, it is almost always the case that more opportunities to improve the business present themselves. Day by day, little by little, the business is transformed from a poorly performing organization to one that is getting results.

▶ *Are you and your team working hard or trying to have fun?*

End The Debate . . . Decide

I think business debate is good. But I am a product of my early career environment. I spent the first 10 years of my career at Unisys Corporation. Unisys was predominantly an engineering company. Open debate was common, vigorous, and expected. You could disagree with the CEO as long as you did so respectfully and with the goal of finding the best answer.

After 10 years in that environment I moved to LensCrafters. For me, it was culture shock. The style that had earned me promotions and achievement awards at Unisys was neither welcome nor appreciated. Open debate was frowned upon. The culture respected and expected behind-the-scenes consensus building. Executive meetings were much more about ratification than vigorous debate.

Which approach is better? They both have their strengths and weaknesses. While the decision-making process at LensCrafters tended to be time-consuming, once a decision was reached the force of the entire organization was devoted to its execution. Everyone was committed to the goal, and it showed. The company set big goals and generally achieved them. At times, however, the need to satisfy so many constituents meant that the decision was less than optimal. At Unisys, decisions were reached more quickly and without extended negotiations. That made it easier to set direction. But at times, after-the-fact negotiations could hamper execution and limit organizational effectiveness.

As with many things in life, balance is the key. There is room for open debate, but only to a point. There are times when debate clearly becomes obstructionist and does not further the organization's goals. At times like this, it is up to leadership to step in and end the debate.

Whether you are in a leadership role or a participant in the debate, ask yourself whether it is serving the organization's goals or some other interest.

As I write this, we are in an economic downturn, and it is more critical than ever for companies to act clearly and decisively. As you participate in or lead the decision-making process at your organization, it's important to consider how long and hard to debate an issue. Once all opinions are heard, there is a point where the organization is better served by moving forward in a definite direction rather than languishing without a decision.

▶ *End the debate. Decide.*

About The Author

Homza's outstanding leadership as a fractional CFO has brought significant financial strength to a broad spectrum of companies where his guidance and expertise allow each of his companies to focus on core business issues.

Ken's experience spans positions with large, billion dollar corporations, mid-range companies and start-up ventures in technology, manufacturing, distribution, retail and service delivery organizations. His résumé includes successful tenures at Unisys and LensCrafters where he served in finance, marketing and strategic roles.

Ken is a financial steward who brings a "spend it like it's your own" approach and has served over 30 clients in various phases of development across multiple industries since 2003. His guidance and expertise cause business owners to have a better understanding of the financial position of their company and improved bottom line results.

For new businesses, he applies his critical thinking to the issues faced during the start-up phase. For more mature businesses, he helps them to better understand their financial results through key performance metrics and financial planning and forecasting while he focuses the executive team on actions to improve profitability. One of the key tenets of Ken's approach is to get to the facts—he believes a better outcome always results from a clear understanding of the actual operating environment as opposed to assumptions and hearsay.

Results have included finding six-figure savings in a matter of weeks, seven-figure profit improvements from one year to the next, and complete business transformations.

He has worked on both sides of the acquisition table, helped two clients through the difficult process of Chapter 11, and served in the dual role of CFO/CEO for a company facing multiple challenges leading it to a successful sale within 15 months of taking the helm.

In addition to serving his clients, Ken has served on various not-for-profit boards and has spoken on finance, strategy and start-up issues in front of business leaders and at the university level.

Ken holds an MBA from the Carnegie Mellon University Tepper School of Business. He and his family reside in University City, Missouri. Learn more about Ken's unique approach at homza.com.

18936807R00119

Printed in Poland
by Amazon Fulfillment
Poland Sp. z o.o., Wrocław